Indian Folklore

Indian Folklore

Being a Collection of Tales
Illustrating the Customs and Manners
of the Indian People

Ganeshji Jethabhai

DK PRINTWORLD
Publishers of Indian Traditions

Cataloging in Publication Data — DK
[Courtesy: D.K. Agencies (P) Ltd. <docinfo@dkagencies.com>]

Kautakamāḷā ane bodhavacana. English.
Indian folklore : being a collection of tales illustrating the customs and manners of the Indian people / Ganeshji Jethabhai.
pages cm
"Story book named as "Kautakamaḷā" aur "bodhavacana", first published in 1885 in Gujarati. English translation ... published by him in Limbdi, Gujarat in 1903" – Title page verso.
ISBN 9788124612408

1. Tales – India – Gujarat. 2. Gujarat (India) – Folklore.
I. Jethabhai, Ganesh, editor, translator. II. Title.

LCC GR305.K38 2024 | DDC 398.20954 23

ISBN: 978-81-246-1240-8
Story book named as "Kautakamāḷā" aur "Bodhavacana"
first published in 1885 in Gujarati.
English translation by Ganeshji Jethabhai, and published by him in Limbdi, Gujarat in 1903
This retypeset edition published in 2024

Printed and published by:
D.K. Printworld (P) Ltd.
Regd. Office: "Vedaśrī", F-395, Sudarshan Park
(Metro Station: ESI Hospital), New Delhi - 110015
Phones: (011) 4172 2626, 98713 94815
e-mail: indology@dkprintworld.com
Website: www.dkprintworld.com

To

His Highness

Sir Jasvantsinhji, K.C.I.E.,

Thakore Saheb of Limbdi

Who is one of the Enlightened Ruling Chiefs of India and who has visited Europe and America.

This book, which is intended to give an insight to the West into the customs and manners of the East, is, with gracious permission, dedicated in token of His travels over the two continents, and His having the proud privilege of being well known to those mighty nations,

by His most faithful and loyal subject, the author.

The book was first published in 1885 CE in Gujarātī and warmly welcomed by the Press and the public and was also sanctioned as a prize and library book by the Director of Public Instruction. Since then it has been thrice reprinted and almost all the copies have been sold. "Mr. Ganeshji", says the Indian Spectator, "has shown considerable skill in shifting and arranging the rude materials collected from many sources and in investigating half forgotten local chronicles of wit and humour with an interest which will give them a permanent place in the literature of the province".

The late Mr. J.W.A. Weir, Collector of Surat and other Englishmen of my acquaintance, who have read my book, advised me to publish an English translation of the same. Acting upon their advice, I got a few stories translated into English and sent them round for opinions which were, without any exceptions, very favourable. "I would certainly encourage you", says the Hon. Mr. Justice Crowe of the Bombay High Court, "to get the book translated into English as it may prove of use to students of Gujarati and will give an insight into the methods of thoughts of the people." It is hoped, therefore, that this English edition of the book will promote a larger acquaintance with and a heartier appreciation of, the native thoughts and native customs, the practical wisdom and ripe experience depicted in the following pages. This is, I think, the first Gujarātī book of its type, translated into English and, if, as such, it forms an interesting and amusing reading for the English knowing people, I shall feel myself amply rewarded.

The Hindi edition of the book is in the Press, and I hope to publish Marāṭhī and Beṅgālī translations of the same very soon.

The work of translation was entrusted to my friend Mr.

Nagardas Malji Dhruva of the Gondal Grasia College, to whom my grateful thanks are due for his hearty cooperation.

I must not also forget to express my sense of obligation to Mr. John F. Hartin, Principal of the said College, for kindly looking over the manuscript and making valuable suggestions.

Limbdi
October 1903

Ganeshji Jethabhai

Contents

ruin or death. A bat cannot see during the daytime; is that any fault of the sun? (*Gulistān of Sheikh Saadi*)

Story 2

A Buffalo in the Bazaar and a Quarrel at Home

In one of the villages of Kāṭhiāwāṛ lived a cultivator named Pāñcho. The name of his wife was Fūlān. One day, when she went out to fetch water, she saw a herd of buffaloes at the village gate and the villagers buying them and driving them home. Fūlān also wanted to buy one and on reaching home she said to her husband, "Do you hear? Splendid buffaloes are being sold dirt cheap at the gate. Go and buy me one this instant. Don't you know that we have long been doing without good milk or whey?"

"Why, woman", said the husband, "I am not blind to it. I will at once go and bring one home; but you will have to give my sister daily as much whey as she requires and that too without mixing much water with it Do you see?"

"That I won't. I have to work hard from morn till night, feeding the buffalo and cleaning the yard; and then to give away whey to *your* brothers and sisters! Why shouldn't I give it to *mine?* Why should they have precedence?"

"You termagant", angrily exclaimed Pāñcho, "dare to do that and I will knock out your brains."

"Let me see you do it. It is easier said than done."

This was too much for Pāñcho. Taking a thick bamboo-stick that was lying by, he made a free use of it on the back of his spouse. The loud lamentations of Fūlān attracted the whole neighbourhood to the scene of action. It was soon found out that the couple had agreed to buy a buffalo, but had disagreed as to the distribution of whey among their relatives after they had bought it, and that was why they had come to blows! A shrewd Baniā named Chaturdās, who was a silent witness of all that had happened, now came forward and thus addressed the couple, "I say, your buffalo has damaged the wall of my house; get it repaired this instant and then there will be time enough to settle the question of whey!" Simultaneously they exclaimed, "We don't own any buffalo; how is it possible then for her to have damaged your wall? "When you have no buffalo", replied the Baniā, "what is this fuss about?" This witty remark brought them to their senses and they retired to their house amid the jeers of the villagers.

Moral: Were it not for the folly and thoughtlessness of human nature, the world would go on very smoothly and half the causes of complaint would disappear.

Story 3

I Will Dip It and Eat It!

A Mahommedan named Sheikh Husain was one day going to a neighbouring village. At midday he reached a pond and as it was very hot, he spread a cloth beneath a banyan tree that was standing on the bank and lay down with the intention of taking a few hours' rest. By chance, another Musalmān came that way and seated himself beside the Sheikh.

Mahommedans as a class are great gossips. They were encouraged to exercise this trait of theirs by the cool breeze and the refreshing shade of the tree overhead. After mutual salaming and inquiry about each other's health, the Sheikh exclaimed, "Allah is all-powerful. To Him nothing is impossible. He can reduce a king to poverty and raise a *fakīr* to a throne in the twinkling of an eye! He can turn a molehill into a mountain immediately. If He would be pleased to transform the leaves of this tree into [2]*roṭīs* and the water of the pond into [3]*ghee*, I would at once pick up *roṭīs*, dip them into the *ghee* and eat them with great pleasure!" The other on hearing this cried out, "Sheikh Sāheb, we are both sitting under the same tree and have therefore equal right to the *roṭīs* and the *ghee*!" "By all means", replied the Sheikh. "I am glad you have admitted it", said the other, "but I do not in the least approve of the extravagant process of dipping. That would soon exhaust our stock of *ghee*. I can't allow more than a spoonful for every cake. You seem to me a great spendthrift!" "But it won't cost us a pie", retorted the Sheikh, "why not then use it freely." At this the other lost temper and exclaimed, "Take care what you are doing; do not trifle with me." "I don't care a fig for you, you miser; I am more than a match for you, do you see?"

From words they came to blows. A few travellers who were going that way were attracted to the place by the noise and on learning the cause of their quarrel, one of them said, "Let the

---

[2] *Roṭīs* = cakes.

[3] *Ghee* = clarified butter.

transformation take place first and there will be time enough to settle the dispute afterwards." This timely remark brought them to their senses and made them ashamed of themselves.

Story 4

Make 50 Cakes out of 4 lbs. of Flour and Give one between the Two. They may Eat as much of It as they can and are Welcome to take Home what is Left!

There lived in Broach a Musalmān named Daulatkhān. He belonged to a noble family which had been reduced by hard times and folly to very poor circumstances. Daulatkhān earned with great pains about 5 rupees per month and this together with his wife's income, derived from grinding corn and spinning cotton, hardly sufficed to keep the wolf from the door. They had, moreover, an only son whom it was necessary they should marry; but they had not a pie to spend on the marriage, nor could they find an obliging Mārwāṛī who would accomodate them even at exorbitant interest. All their friends and relations, to the number of about one hundred, must be invited to dinner on the occasion, yet they had nothing in the house of any value, or they would have gladly disposed of it or mortgaged it. On ran-sacking the whole house, however, they found about 4 lbs. of wheat which they resolved to sacrifice for this grand occasion.

"You grind the wheat", said the Moslem to his wife, "and make 50 cakes of the flour. In the meantime I will go and invite our friends and relatives. When they come and sit down to dinner, you serve one cake between two and tell them plainly that they may eat as much of it as they can and are welcome to carry home what is left!" "I never heard of guests being allowed to take the food home; it is enough if we feed them. Even [4]*sāhūkār*s do no more!" suggested the [5]Bībī thoughtfully. "Such is the custom in our family. I don't care what others do and how much they spend. I can afford to be liberal on an occasion like this which does not occur very often. I must and will keep up the prestige of my worthy ancestors!"

The cakes were accordingly prepared and the guests began to pour in. When they wore seated and served with half a cake each (weighing about half an ounce), they were at a loss to decide how much of it to eat and how much to take home for children! Not to give offence to the host and to show him that the food was more than enough, they cut the bread into two pieces, ate one and carried home the other!

When all had departed except a few select friends, Daulatkhān asked his wife to bring some food for himself and children. When he was told, however, that there was not a morsel of food in the house, he cried out, "What I had not these fellows had sense enough to leave some food even for the children? It is fortunate that my friends are here and they will gladly resign their share to the children, I am sure!" The friends appealed to, had to surrender the bread, go home and make what arrangements they could for their dinner!

---

4 *Sāhūkārs* = Rich people.

5 *Bībī* = A Mahommedan lady.

Moral:

Of all the causes which conspire to blind
Man's erring judgement and misguided mind
What the weak head with strongest bias rules
Is pride the never failing vice of fools.

Story 5

Dragging the Well

A wealthy barber of Wadhwān invited all his caste-fellows, living within a radius of 12 miles from the town, to a caste-dinner. The assemblage was so great that everywhere, inside and outside the town, none but barbers were to be found. A group of these village-surgeons was comfortably seated on the steps leading down to a well and gossiping on indifferent topics, when a happy and quite novel idea struck one of them. Addressing his fellows he exclaimed, "There is no well in our village. If we can, therefore, contrive to carry this one there, we should confer a great boon on the villagers."

"That is a happy idea", said another barber. "With our united force it would be easy enough to carry it with us. When [6]Hanumān could carry a big mountain in the palm of his hand, there is no reason why we, who are so many, should not drag a well after us."

"Mere words won't do", said another. "Do you suggest any

[6] Hanumān = The monkey God.

means of achieving the feat? You can't shave before you have wetted the hair, you know." To this the second barber replied, "Let us buy sufficient ropes to drag it with"; but another interposed with "Where is the money to buy them with? If you can do it without spending a pie, do it; not otherwise." A barber who appeared to be thinking deeply, then made the following suggestion: "Listen to me. We have with us razors and scissors. Let us cut-off our hair and weave it into a rope." To this the originator of the scheme replied, "You are an ass. It would take a long time to weave the hair into a rope. I propose that all present should give up their turbans for the purpose which when tied together would form a long rope. Tie one end of it to one of the pillars of the well and pull at the other with all your strength."

The last proposal seemed the most feasible and the least expensive. All present took off their turbans which were soon formed into a long rope. Then they fastened one end of it to a pillar of the well and began to pull at the other with all their might; but the turbans could not stand the strain and with a creaking noise, which the silly fellows interpreted as due to the motion of the well, they were torn asunder and down came the barbers with a crash, some breaking their bones while others escaped with slight injury! Thoroughly ashamed of their folly, they at once took the nearest road to their village, bare-headed and smeared with blood.

Moral:

Attempt not impossibilities.
Sure of all follies this the greatest is
Madly to attempt impossibilities.
Cf. The Viper and the file — *Aesop's Fables.*

Story 6

Who Says It is a [7]Rāmpi Cut?

At one end of a street in Jāmnagar, stood the shop of a cobbler named Premlā. The cattle of half the town passed and repassed by his shop twice a day — once in the early morning when they went out to graze and once in the evening when they were driven home for the night. Among the cattle there was a fat and mischievous buffalo. She was a great nuisance to the children of the street, as no sooner did she catch sight of them, than she rushed at them with raised tail and lowered head. She was always ready for a fight, and failing to find a combatant, she would rub her back against every wall in the street and thrust her horns in every doorway by which she passed. She would really have made a name and won a prize if she were allowed to take part in a bull-fight in Spain or an elephant-fight in Barodā.

Now this wilful buffalo had made it a rule to rub her back against Premlā's wall every time she passed by his shop, and in so doing she often damaged it and put poor Premlā to the expense of getting it repaired.

One morning when Premlā was at work, the buffalo passed by his shop and rubbed her back against the newly-repaired wall, as was her habit and brought it down with a crash. Premlā was heartily tired of her mischievous pranks and with the fixed intention of teaching her a lesson, he seized a *rāmpi* that was lying by and ran after her. Before the buffalo had gone very far, he inflicted a deep wound on her neck and returned to his

[7] *Rāmpi* = A cobbler's knife.

shop well pleased with the result, the more so, as none had observed him while he struck the blow.

A short time after, when the people began to stir out of their houses, they found the buffalo lying in the street and, weltering in the blood that had flowed copiously from the wound. A crowd of persons of all castes and creeds was soon formed round her body and everybody was advancing his own theory regarding the nature of the wound and the instrument with which it was made.

"It seems to be," said a barber, "the work of an idler, who has got no better work to do. It reminds me of a barber out of work who plied his razor on the back of a young buffalo when human beings were beyond his reach!"

"You are every inch a barber," remarked a Baniā, "and there is no sense in what you say. Because a man has nothing to do, it does not follow that he would wantonly take the life of a buffalo. There must be some deep motive in this act."

"It must have been so written in her forehead", said an astrologer. "Even Brahmā cannot check or alter the course of Destiny. What is done is done. There is no use talking about it." To this a cultivator replied, "That won't do. What if we have to turn the whole field upside down? The culprit must be found out and put in the stocks. Nothing less would save our cattle from further molestation."

"I quite agree with you", said an oilman. "The murder will out, as does a drop of oil from the bottom of a bucket full of water."

"Ten to one," remarked a woodcutter, "it is the work of someone living in this street. We had, therefore, better enquire in the neighbourhood; for, you all know that the handle of an axe is the destruction of its progenitor."

"I am not sure of that," doubtfully exclaimed a tailor; "why do not the neighbours come forward and give out the truth. They all seem to be in league against the poor buffalo. There is no patching of the sky if it is ever torn." To this a carpenter agreed and added, "They require a boring. We had better hand them all over to the Police and then the real culprit would surely be detected." "I am of the same opinion", put in a Miān. "Kick and then question is my policy which if followed would surely bring out the truth."

"That strikes me as an excellent suggestion", said a goldsmith. "Test pure gold in whatever way you like, it would never blacken. Likewise, those who are innocent will come out unhurt." "If you have made up your minds," remarked a widow, "why waste time? 'Long a widow weds with shame'. " "You all know," said a prostitute, "that what belongs to the public belongs to nobody. I, therefore, propose that you form a committee and authorize them to take necessary steps. A bastard is the son of no man!"

"The last bed is watered," impatiently exclaimed a gardener, "that is the buffalo is dead. Do what you will, but do it soon."

"This is sailing over smooth waters. I wonder how you would manage if you had to sail over rough seas!" testily remarked a sailor. A Vohorā who had some experience of law courts said, "You people don't know what going to law means. You will be asked when, where and by whom the buffalo was seen alive last, why did you not report the matter at once and whom do you suspect. Then you will have to give your evidence on oath and undergo a searching cross-examination. Why take all this responsibility upon your heads for nothing? Think before you act."

"I don't quite understand," said a shepherd, "what you all mean. God has given you two hands and strength enough to use them. Why not find out the murderer and dispatch him at once? That is the way to end the matter."

The shepherd's advice was disregarded and it was decided by an overwhelming majority to report the matter to the Police, when a trio consisting of an old Arab pensioner, a Rājpūt and a Habshi arrived on the spot. They were severally asked to examine the wound and say with what instrument it was inflicted. After carefully examinning the wound the Arab said, "Inasmuch as it is not straight, it seems to have been inflicted by a scimitar and must therefore be the work of an Arab such as generally wear that weapon." "I beg your pardon," exclaimed the Habshi, "the wound is quite straight and deep. She must have fallen a victim to the long knife of a Habshi beggar who may have some private grudge against her owner." "I am a better authority in such cases," said the Rājpūt; "It is decidedly a wound inflicted by a battleaxe which Rājpūts alone know how to wield."

This difference of opinion as regards the nature of the wound led to further discussion on the subject. An old gardener, who had not uttered a word till now, came forward and after examining the wound, he said, "I am prepared to declare it on oath, if need be, that this wound is inflicted by a scraper". Some of the bystanders did not understand what he meant by a scraper. They asked him what it was like, to which he replied that it resembled a cobbler's knife or *rāmpi* as they call it.

Premlā, who had joined the group and was attentively

listening to their discussion, was startled at the words "cobbler and *rāmpi*" and his guilty conscience led him to believe that the truth had at last come out and that he would soon be arrested and dragged to the *darbār*. He, therefore, put on a bold face which was, however, belied by his chattering teeth and trembling body. He bounded forward and seizing the gardener by the wrist, he exclaimed, "Who says it is a *rāmpi* cut? Who saw me doing it and when?"

This voluntary though inadvertent confession convinced the spectators that Premlā was the guilty person. The matter was, however, amicably settled, the cobbler agreeing to pay a sufficient compensation to the owner of the buffalo.

Moral:

Truth crushed to earth shall rise again
The eternal years of God are hers.

Story 7

A Hundred Snakes in a Bush

The villagers were sitting one evening on the [8]*chorā*, when Faskū who had been out for a walk came running towards them breathless and sank down by their side without uttering a word. After allowing him to rest for a while, one of his friends asked him what had made him run so hard. "Thank God!" said Faskū, "Were it not for Him, I should have

[8] *Chorā* = Public place in a village.

been a dead man long ago." "Really!" exclaimed his friends simultaneously. "Tell us what it was." "I had wearied myself to death with a brisk walk of several miles, when on seeing Mādhā Patel's farm at hand, I entered it and stretched my limbs under the cool shade of the *nīm*-tree. I had hardly done so when I heard a rustling noise in the neighbouring bush. On looking round I saw something like a hundred snakes with their mouths wide open. They would have bitten me to death and eaten me all up, had I not made the best use of my legs. If it were one of you instead of me, you would have been frightened to death, I am sure! but I am no coward, you know!"

"We have seen the place and all the bushy places around it", said one of his friends. "There is not a single bush large enough to hold a hundred snakes. We can't believe you, my friend. There must be some mistake as regards the number."

"Well," said Faskū, "if you think a hundred are too many, I am sure they were not less than fifty or sixty."

"Too small a place to contain so many", replied his friend. "Try to form as correct an estimate as you can and then let us know it." "They were crowded together," rejoined Faskū, "so it was not easy to count them all. However they were not less than twenty-five I can assure you."

"This district," said his friend, "does not abound in snakes. Again snakes are not very social creatures and so they do not move in companies. We seldom find them together. Do not exaggerate facts, my friend, but tell us the plain truth."

"As you say they do not live much together," replied Faskū, "the number must be less. What if I say there were five or six of them."

"Still we can't believe you. Take out the percentage you may have added and give us the net result."

"There must have been one at least. There is no doubt about that."

"Must have been or must have not been is not the question. Tell us how many you saw with your own eyes."

Being thus hard pressed, Faskū gave way and said, "To tell you the truth, I did not see even one! But then, how do you account for that rustling noise otherwise?"

To this the assembled villagers rejoined, "You are a very brave man, indeed! When mere noise frightens you so much, what would you do if confronted by a real snake?"

Moral: The credit got by a lie only lasts till the truth comes out.

Story 8

Sluggards who Prefer Death to Work

One of the emperors of Delhi was one day passing through the streets of the city, when his eyes fell on three beggars who were all in rags and whose faces were covered with swarms of flies. On inquiry the emperor learnt that they were too lazy to help themselves. He ordered some food for them, but they would not hold out their hands to receive it. It was forcibly thrust into their mouths and it was with great trouble that they could be prevailed upon to swallow it. The emperor thought to himself that if he left them to their fate, they would succumb to a painful and lingering death and so he ordered his vizier to take them to a government building and look after them. They were accordingly placed on a bullock cart and conducted to a building which was set apart for them and which was styled "The Castle of Indolence". A number of attendances was then employed to look after them and help them in every way. Then a Royal proclamation was issued to the effect that sluggards of every description would be freely admitted to the castle and supplied with free board and lodging.

Fortunately for the poor it happened to be the year of a disastrous famine and many a beggar contrived to get admission to the castle by feigning indolence. In a short time the castle was overcrowded with occupants and so-called sluggards were everyday pouring in from all parts of the empire. The daily expenses of keeping up such an institution were very high and the emperor was at a loss to find a way out of the difficulty. He summoned his vizier who was a shrewd man and asked him to devise some means of getting rid of the false sluggards.

The vizier accordingly repaired to the castle and ordered the superintendent to have a hedge of dry thorns made all round the building, leaving space for a small footpath in front of the castle. When the hedge was ready, the vizier ordered his men to set it on fire. The so-called sluggards seeing the whole compound ablaze were thrown into confusion and to save their lives they fled pell-mell leaving the whole of the building vacant!

The emperor and the vizier then entered the castle to see if any of its former inmates were left within. To their surprise they found, all the rooms deserted except one in which were lying those three sluggards for whom the castle was originally opened. When the emperor and the vizier entered the room, they heard one of the sluggards saying to his companions, "Look there, my friends, the fire is rapidly progressing towards our room. It has been long burning and does not seem to be exhausted as yet." "I am not going to put myself to the unnecessary trouble of opening my eyes!" leisurely replied the second. "Can't you both be quiet?" angrily exclaimed the third.

The emperor was surprised to find that there were persons on the face of the earth who would not exert themselves a little to save their lives! He was so much disgusted by their conduct that he asked them what they lived for if life was such a burden to them. To this they replied, "Even death would cost us some exertion which we are not prepared to undergo. That is why we live!"

Moral: The curse of sloth makes a man a burden to himself and to others and his life is simply miserable.

Story 9

Too Lazy to Pick Up Berries

A sluggard was one day quietly lying under a bore-tree (jujube tree). At a little distance from him, but quite within his reach, lay a few ripe berries. The sluggard longed to have them, but he did not like to put himself to the trouble of extending his hand for the purpose. He therefore made up his mind to apply for help to the first passerby.

After waiting thus for about half an hour, he saw a traveller, mounted on a camel going at full speed, pass by the tree. The sluggard asked him to stop for a while and reach him the berries. The traveller, greatly surprised at the odd request, said, "My friend, you do not seem to have thought what inconvenience and waste of time it would cause me to stop the camel, make it sit down, get down from it, collect the berries, put them into your mouth and then remount the camel! The berries are lying quite within your reach and you have only to stretch out your hand to get them. Why don't you do it?" "You are a great sluggard," said the lazy fellow. "You are no good. Go your own way. I will apply to some other person less lazy than yourself."

The traveller left the place greatly amused.

Moral: No one is willing to help a person who does not help himself. To do so would be lost labour — a writing upon water, a sowing upon sand.

Story 10

[9]Kaṅkoḍī is Cleared Off by Worms, Soap is Rotten, Iron is Eaten up by Mice and Hūrbāi is Carried Away by a Kite

There was once a great merchant named Adamji Mullāh living in Cambay who dealt in a variety of goods both on his own account and also in the capacity of a commission

[9] *Kaṅkoḍī* = A kind of white powder.

agent. As Cambay was a thriving seaport at the time and things from different parts of the country were imported for sale, Adamji soon made a fortune and established a sound reputation as an honest dealer.

One day, a Baniā residing in a far-off corner of India, arrived at his shop, bringing with him bags of *kaṅkoḍī*, boxes of soap and cart-loads of iron. Adamji accorded him a cordial reception and assured him that he would do what he could to dispose of the commodities at prices that would bring him a large profit. The samples were shown to intending buyers, but the rates they offered were too low to be accepted. The Baniā, therefore, instructed the Mullāh to sell the things when prices were higher and leaving the goods with him, he went to his native place.

After a few months, the rates of all the three articles left by the Baniā rose very high. The Mullāh, consequently, sold off the goods and collected and kept the cash to be paid to the Baniā at some future date. On account of some unavoidable circumstances the Baniā, could not call for the money for a very long time. This neglect on his part induced the wily Mullāh to misappropriate the sum. Adamji debited the sum to the Baniā's account as if it were paid off and squared the account.

After a few years had elapsed, the Baniā came to Cambay and went directly to Adamji's shop and said, "Well, Mullāh Sāheb, I hope you have disposed of the articles I left with you. Let us settle the account if you have". Adamji knowing well that if he showed the account books the false entry would be detected, began to beat about the bush that he might gain time to find out a plausible excuse by which the Baniā might be deceived. He, therefore, said, "I wish you had come earlier. I am sorry the idea of calling you in time did not strike me. I am very sorry, indeed!" "Why," replied the Baniā, "should you be sorry, my friend? Have you sold them at a loss? Or do any of the buyers refuse to pay?"

"That is not it. I am extremely sorry it should have so happened."

"Then what is it? I can't understand word of what you say."

Adamji then said, "Your things would have fetched a very good price and left you a big margin; 'but the hare springs out when one least expects it'. Under your own eye, the things were heaped in my warehouse. Six months ago, when I went there to show samples thereof to a customer, I found the *kaṅkoḍī* eaten up by worms, the soap rotten and the iron eaten up by mice! Several other articles belonging to me were also heaped along with yours and they too were damaged. But I don't claim any compensation from you, for, I know that you have already suffered very heavily!"

The Baniā was too shrewd to be taken in like that. The Mullāh's statement appeared to him quite absurd. The trick to rob him of his due was too transparent to deceive him. He, however, put on a serious look and said, "Well, you need not be sorry for what has happened, though I quite fail to see how it did happen. But it sometimes does occur that 'Likely lies in the mire when unlikely get over'."

The Baniā then hired rooms in the vicinity of Adamji's house and stayed there waiting for an opportunity to recover the money with interest from the dishonest Mullāh. One day when the Mullāh's little girl was playing in the street he called her, took her to one of his rooms, gave her some toys and sweetmeats and went about his own business quietly awaiting the result.

It began to grow dark and the girl did not return home. The parents grew anxious and Adamji inquired at every house she was in the habit of frequenting, but she was nowhere to be found. Quite overcome by fatigue, he was returning home at midnight, when the Baniā called him and asked him if anything unusual had happened. The Mullāh related the mysterious disappearance of his daughter and asked him if he had seen her in the evening. To this the Baniā replied, "I am sorry to inform you that I saw her being carried by a kite! The poor girl was crying piteously and I tried all I could to free her from its grasp, but in vain!" "It is absurd", said the Mullāh. "Why do you make fun of me?" "Upon my word, I tell you that I saw her with my own eyes!" replied the Baniā.

As a thief is ever fancying the moon is up, so did the Mullāh at once guess that it was the Baniā's work and that he had kidnapped the girl to serve his own purpose. Next morning he went to the Kāẓī and lodged a complaint against the Baniā. The judge summoned the accused and asked him if he had seen Adamji's girl. The Baniā replied, "Yes, your worship, I saw her being carried away by a kite last evening; and I said so to my friend in reply to his inquiry."

"Absurd!" said the Kāẓī. "I can't believe you." "Why, your worship," retorted the Baniā, "you can ask my friend and he will tell you that more absurd things have happened before now. To quote an instance: I left a few bags of *kaṅkoḍī*, several boxes of soap and a quantity of iron with Adamji for disposal a few years ago. When I asked him for payment, he told me that the first was cleared off by worms, the second was petrified and the third was eaten up by mice! In a place where worms and mice are so gigantic as to eat up *kaṅkoḍī* and iron and digest them, it is not to be wondered at if the kites carry away young children! There is nothing absurd in it!"

The judge asked Adamji whether the Baniā's statement was true and on learning that it was, he ordered the Mullāh's books to be brought into the court and examined and the full amount that he owed to the Baniā to be paid down there and then. Hūrbāi was then handed over to her loving father who quietly went home.

Moral: Deceit deserves to be deceived. The lesson taught is the necessity of keeping within the prescribed bounds of morality.

Cf. The dog and the wolf.
The Eagle and the fox. } *Aesop's Fables.*

Story 11

The Long and Short of a Thing

A Mahommedan and a Baniā, who were great friends, passed much of their time together, and had no secrets from each other. It happened that both were orphans. One day when they were sitting together, the Baniā asked his friend how his father had died. "My father went to a garden, one day," said the Musalmān, "and climbed a tree. As he was swinging to and fro, from the topmost branch, it suddenly gave way and my father fell down dead on the ground. Now tell me of what did your father die?"

"My father," replied the Baniā, "was carried off in prime

of life. On the evening of his 30th birthday, he ate too many sweetmeats which caused indigestion and that in its turn brought on fever. The temperature was so high that he became quite unconscious and would neither take food nor talk to anybody. There was a burning sensation all over the body and his tongue clove to the roof of his mouth. This gave him a sore throat and made us all very anxious about him. We had to sit by his bed day and night and had, besides, to attend to all our relatives and friends who came from distant places to see him."..."How did it all end?" Impatiently demanded his friend. "I am coming to that presently", said the Baniā. "We tried various medicines, but they did him no good. We then called in Vithlā Barber who, as you know, is reputed to be the best physician in our town, but he too could do nothing. We then thought that perhaps a ghost was troubling him, so the persons who could repeat charms and drive away the evil spirits were summoned; but they too gave up the case as hopeless. Medicines and [10]*mantras* were alike useless."

"My friend," interrupted the Mahommedan, "you are becoming more and more tedious. When will your father die? Let me know that." "Everything," replied the Baniā, "will come in its proper place. Be patient. I have not yet done with the symptoms. The temperature rose higher and higher and at last it rose to 106°. Consciousness then forsook him and he began to rave like a mad man. We had his head bathed in rose-water, but that did not allay the fever a bit. We then gave him a cold bath, which instead of doing him any good, brought on pneumonia. Every moment the symptoms grew worse and more alarming. A few hours had thus elapsed when his strength began to give

10 *Mantras* = Charms.

way. His hands and feet grew icy cold. He could not hear what we said and his eyesight began to fail. The end, it seemed, was speedily approaching and we thought it was high time to read to him religious [11]*ślokas* and give what we could in charities that might stand him in good stead in the next world and entitle him to a place in the [12]*svarga*. Then ...".

The Mahommedan who was quite tired of listening to the story which he thought would never end, exclaimed, "Why don't you cut it short and say that the fever killed him? That, I think, is the long and short of it."

"You asked me," said the Baniā, "how my father died and I was telling you what had actually happened. If you are in a hurry, we will talk about it some other time."

Moral: Avoid always the roundabout way of telling a story. Let your answers be short and to the point.

Story 12

To be Very Liberal with Other People's Money

There lived a Vohorā named Mūsābhāī in Siddhapur, who belonged to a good family and had once been very rich; but a great loss in trade had greatly impoverished him. He was, with great difficulty, living from hand to mouth,

---

11 *Ślokas* = Verses.

12 *Svarga* = Heaven.

when his father died, on which occasion his caste fellows had to be fed, whether he could afford it or not. Mūsābhāi was a sensible man and he, therefore, did not think it safe to incur a debt that would cripple him for life, in order to feed people who would speak well of him for a few days and then leave him to take care of himself as best as he could. When his relatives and the leading persons of the [13]*jamāt* came to know of his resolve, they went to him and said, "A father's death and a wife's first pregnancy do not occur twice in one's lifetime. Both the occasions must, therefore, be duly celebrated. Again, you come of a family who are well known for their generosity and you should not tarnish their fair name by falling short of your duty on the present occasion."

Mūsābhāī thought to himself that the fellows ought to be taught a lesson and with this object in view, he expressed his willingness to follow their advice and a day was fixed for feeding the *jamāt*.

Every community in all towns have a number of cooking pots and dishes of brass which are lent out to those who intend giving caste-dinners, as a private individual cannot possibly have vessels enough for an occasion like this. Mūsābhāī, therefore, borrowed all the brass and copper pots, secretly mortgaged them for about 1,000 rupees and bought flour, *ghee*, sugar and other articles required for the occassion.

On the appointed day the whole community sat down to dinner and a variety of sweetmeats was served to them. Mūsābhāī, with a fan in one hand and a cup of cold water in the other, was moving from dish to dish and was pressing everyone to do full justice to the homely fare, as he called it. The guests

---

[13] *Jamāt* = Musalmān community.

were loud in their praises of the generosity of the host, to which the latter promptly and appropriately replied, "It is very kind of you to say so, but it is all your own, my friends; nothing is mine except water and air!" The guests could not understand the deep and hidden meaning conveyed in the reply and ascribed it to Mūsābhāi's modesty and good breeding. After dinner all went home, much pleased with the entertainment.

Many days passed but Mūsābhāī did not return the vessels he had borrowed. When the person in whose charge they were kept went to him and asked for the vessels, Mūsābhāi cooly replied, "I told the *jamāt* to their very faces that what they were eating was their own and not mine. I spoke the truth when I said so, for, it was with the money that their vessels fetched, that I purchased articles of food and fed them. I have not, however, sold them, but simply mortgaged them. If the *jamāt* want them, they are welcome to pay the 1,000 rupees with interest to banker so and so and take back the vessels." The *jamāt* had to raise fund to pay the banker and from that time they gave up meddling with other people's business.

Moral: It is a custom and a very ruinous one among the natives of India to spend extravagently on death and marriage occasions. Not only do they not provide for their children, but often leave them heavy debts to pay.

It is a suicidal policy to waste what little we have; for, requirements of old age and need of rest, are things inevitable and ought to be provided for.

Story 13

Why do They go to Mālwā? They Might as well Stay at Home and Eat [14]Khājā and Sugar

In times gone by a disastrous famine overtook the province of Gujarat. Owing to the failure of crops, the ryots prepared to emigrate to Mālwā, in the hope of procuring food for themselves and fodder for their cattle. One morning, a number of ryots on their way to Mālwā passed by the royal palace, when the eyes of the crown prince, who was making merry with his friends and feasting on *khājā* and other sweetmeats, fell upon them. He asked one of the attendants where they were going. "They are emigrating to Mālwā," replied the man, "owing to the scarcity of food and fodder here." "Why do they do so?" exclaimed the prince. "They might as well stay at home and eat *khājā* and sugar."

This made them all laugh. One of his friends said, "You are born in gold and purple and do not, therefore, know what hardships these poor people have to undergo in times like these. Persons rolling in wealth and surrounded by luxuries cannot realize the miseries of the poor. Why talk of *khājā* and sugar, when they cannot even get [15]*bājarī* bread and an onion?" The prince could not understand him, so he remarked that if *bājarī* was scarce, they might eat wheat instead!" "*bājarī* or wheat," remarked his friend "does not make any difference. The thing is they have not money to buy either. These people are chiefly dependent on their crops and when they fail, they are reduced

[14] *Khājā* = A kind of sweetmeat.

[15] *Bājarī* = Millet; a sort of food grain.

to helplessness. Unfortunately, we have not opened any "relief works" that they might earn enough to keep body and soul together. There is, therefore, no other help for them but to leave this land and go to Mālwā which is free from famine this year. You may have heard the proverb which says, 'Rain is the mightiest of monarchs who supports the whole world and mother's is the best and most wholesome milk'."

Moral: Secure ourselves, we too often view with indifference the dangers of others, for, none knows the weight of another's burden.

Story 14

All the People of the Town Eat Rice and Milk

The Emperor Akbar had in his court a jester named Lahūwā who was well known for his wit and humour. One day when the emperor was in good humour the jester said, "There are a good many cows and buffaloes in your *darbār*, while most of the people of the town do not even get good milk. Rice of good quality is to be had abundantly, but without fresh and pure milk it is of no use." The emperor divining the jester's meaning asked him whether he was making a personal complaint or one on behalf of the whole town. "I don't live outside the town," replied the jester, "and am therefore included therein." "I can't," said the emperor, "supply the whole town with buffaloes, but if you want one, you can have it." The jester thankfully accepted the offer and drove one of the finest buffaloes to his house.

After a few days the emperor again asked Lahūwā, how the people were getting on; to which the jester replied, "They are all getting on nicely, your Majesty. They are all eating rice and milk and are quite happy and contented." "The other day," responded Akbar, "you were complaining that good milk was not to be had. I did not supply them all with cows and buffaloes. You were the only person who profited by the complaint. How does it happen then, that they are *all* having good milk?" "It is the world's way, not mine alone, your Majesty! For, he who is warm thinks everyone else is."

Story 15

Allah has Already taken His Due

A [16]*fakīr*, who lived on public charity and made a [17]*masjid* his home, once prayed to Allāh to befriend him, as he was unable to support the pangs of poverty any longer; and vowed that if he got a rupee he would spend a quarter of it in charity and keep three quarters for himself.

As he was one day walking along the streets, he accidentally found a rupee. He was much pleased with his good fortune, but when he remembered his vow, he began to regret that he had made it. On consideration, he bade good-bye to the vow, as his

[16] *Fakīr*, Sāī = A religious mendicant.

[17] *Masjid* = A mosque.

object was attained. With a view to buy some food, he went to a Baniā, to get the rupee changed. The Baniā, after carefully examining the coin, said, "Sāī, the rupee is defaced and of short weight; it will therefore fetch four *ānnā*s less!" The *fakīr* took the rupee to several places, but everywhere he met with the same reply; at last he grew, weary and exclaimed, "Allāh knew that I was not honest and He seems, therefore, to have taken His due, instead of trusting me to pay it!"

Moral: Selfish persons bid good-bye to the basket when grapes are gathered and think they will have no further occasion for it. But the ways of Providence are inscrutable.

Story 16

[18]Gābhā in Place of [19]Gāmbhū

Times are changing and landed properties too change hands every now and then. There was a time when the little village of Gāmbhū in Kāṭhiāwāṛ belonged to tailors and that is why they are known by the nickname of [20]Grāsiās of Gāmbhū even at the present day.

Gāmbhū, when it was in the hands of the tailors, was invaded by a neighbouring Rājpūt prince and the tailors had to surrender to the victor. When the tailors living in other parts of the province heard this sad news, they resolved to recapture

18 Gābhā = Grags.

19 Gāmbhū = Name of a village.

20 Grāsiā = Grāsa or landholder.

the village. With this object in view they sent messengers to every place and in a short time a large body of tailors with [21]*gaẓa* and scissors assembled in the vicinity of Gāmbhū.

Towards the evening, one day, a council of war was held to settle what time would be most convenient for the attack. After a long and hot discussion it was decided that they should pass the night outside the village and at dawn of day, when the gates opened, they should rush into the village and occupy all the important places.

With the firm resolve of attacking the village in the morning, they laid themselves down in a long line beginning from the village gate. They were so many that the line so formed was about a mile in length.

Now the tailor lying nearest the gate thought that he would be the first man to fall into the hands of the enemy in case of a surprise during the night. He, therefore, rose from his place, passed along the line and lay down at the other extremity, thinking himself quite safe there. His neighbour, the second in order, who was watching his movements, did the same. He was followed by the third and so on. Thus they all kept on moving throughout the night. By the time the sun rose next morning, they had receded more than 10 miles from the village!

As was arranged, they prepared for the attack, but neither the village nor its gate were to be seen! Finding themselves in a forest, some of them exclaimed, "What has taken place during the night? We remember to have gone to sleep near the gate of Gāmbhū! Some [22]*deva* or [23]*rākṣasa* must have carried us

---

[21] *Gaẓa* = A measure two feet in length.

[22] *Deva* = A God.

[23] *Rākṣasa* = A demon.

to this place! "At this an old and experienced tailor, who had witnessed the nocturnal march of his brethren, retorted, "My friends, we had better go home and mind our own business. We are all cowards and that is what has moved us all so far from the village."

Being ashamed of their conduct, they quietly went home and began to ply their needles as was their wont? This has given rise to the proverb, "Gābhā in place of Gāmbhū"; which if repeated in the presence of a tailor, at once rouses his anger even at the present day.

Moral: Vain pretenders give themselves hectoring airs and assume to be braver than they really are. Such persons are ever in danger of being discovered and then they are exposed to the ridicule and humiliation of the world.

Cf. The Ass in the Lion's skin.— *Aesop's Fables.*

Story 17

A Fool's Bolt is Soon Shot

A Koli had married a girl whose parents never sent her to his house. Whenever the poor fellow went to bring her home with him, he was flatly told that the girl was unable to walk a step, for, that would take the paint off her feet which were always kept coloured with the *mehandī*-juice.[24]

Failing to gain the consent of her parents either by threats

---

[24] *Mehandī* = *Lawsonia inermis.*

or persuasion, the husband at last thought of carrying her away secretly. With this intention, he went to the town where his father-in-law resided and before executing his project, he informed the leading persons of his caste of his intention. They went with him to the bride's house and persuaded her father to send his daughter with her husband, saying, "It is not safe for a grown up girl to live with her parents. She must either go to her husband's house or to the burning ground. There is no other alternative. If you won't hand her over to her husband at once, we will excommunicate you; and that will bring you into great trouble." The threat of excommunication brought the obstinate father to his senses and he agreed to send her on condition that on no account should the paint on her feet be allowed to wear off. The poor husband agreed and bought a pair of slippers to keep the colour wearing off.

Next morning the couple left the town. At noon they reached the bank of a river. The river must be crossed and that too without washing the paint off her feet! That was a great problem and not an easy one. The fertile brain of the husband, however, found a way out of it. He lifted his bride on his shoulders and loaded with a weight of about 10 stone he began to cross the river. The water grew deeper and deeper and by the time he reached the middle of the stream, it touched her feet. The poor fellow was again in a fix. Anyhow the paint must be preserved and the only way to do it was to hold her head downwards! The woman began to cry piteously, but her husband was mindful only of the stipulation which he made up his mind to fulfil even at the risk of his wife's life! Water began to get into the woman's mouth, ears and nostrils and she was soon strangled.

When he reached the opposite bank, some people who had

watched this strange proceeding, began to reproach the man for his cruel conduct, to which the Koli replied, "You speak thus because you don't know the facts. I had to preserve the paint on her feet at any cost and I have done it. I am not to blame for the result. I have kept my promise to her parents and that is all I care for!"

Moral: Obstinacy tends to make us negligent of approaching peril. Let us beware when engrossed by obstinacy that we do not come to grief.

Cf. — Fools Rush in Where Angels Fear to Tread.

Story 18

Happen What May, I won't Add to It Another Grain

Two [25]Memons of Morvi — uncle and nephew with tin boxes containing false pearls, combs, essences and other small wares, went pedling about the country. When they were returning home after disposing of their goods, they came to a [26]*juwārī*-field at the sight of which the nephew exclaimed, "This is the most fertile soil I ever saw. The ears are bending down under the weight of grain. It will bring in a nice crop to its lucky owner, won't it?"

"That it will," replied his uncle. "How much *juwārī* do you

[25] Memon = A class of Mahommedans.

[26] *Juwārī* = A kind of food grain.

think the field will produce?" "Not less than 120 maunds, I am sure." "You don't mean what you say, do you? For myself, I estimate it at 60 maunds and not a grain more."

"You do injustice to the poor owner by forming too low an estimate of the product."

The uncle getting rather excited, retorted, "Look at my beard, my boy. It has not grown white without bringing to its owner an adequate amount of experience of the world to guide misguided youths like you." "The brains do not lie in the beard, my good sir", replied his nephew hotly. "You are talking, nonsense and no wonder; for, old age is second childhood."

"Wretch," shouted the uncle, "I can't put up with your impudence any longer. Out of my sight, you idiot."

"Take care! Never show your teeth unless you can bite, you old dog. Keep quiet or I shall knock out your brains."

"You urchin," roared the old man; "let me see you do it."

The boy at once took the box off his shoulders, put it on the ground and giving a twist to his mustache, he seized his uncle, who was too weak to withstand the attack, by the beard and brought him to the ground. The old man tried to free himself from the vice-like grip of his nephew, but in repeated attempts to do so, the hair of his beard came out in handfuls. The boy refused to let go his hold unless he admitted that the field would produce not less than 120 maunds of *juwārī*. Regardless of the result and although in imminent danger of losing his venerable heard, the old man exclaimed, "Happen what may; I won't add another grain to it."

Moral: Do not make much ado about nothing.

Story 19

Even a Snake Laid by may have Its Use

Somchand, a Baniā of Barodā, was day and night impressing upon his wife and children that everything, however trivial, has its use and nothing should, therefore, be thrown away as useless. Even dust and ashes he collected and sold them to cultivators for manure.

His children did not like the ways of their father. Once when his eldest son made bold to suggest that he was laughed at and commented upon for his miserly habit, he quietly answered, "Do what you will, when you become the head of the family. What I have been doing is the result of long experience and I mean to stick to it. You talk of dust and ashes being useless rubbish and not worth collecting, but I say that not even a snake laid by is without its use at some proper time. I have nothing to do with the opinion of others and I care not for what they say." "You may be right, father," said the son, "but for myself, I don't quite see the use of a snake laid by." "I will explain it to you when the time comes", replied the father.

One day, the dead body of a snake happened to be lying on the road. The boys picked it up, brought it to their father and asked him to explain to them the use of it. "Throw it on the roof of the house and wait for a few days", said the father.

Now it so happened that the king's wife, one day, went to take a bath on the terrace of the palace; and putting off her clothes and ornaments placed them on a *dīvān* lying by. A kite flying overhead happened to catch sight of her necklace set with lustrous diamonds and taking it for a suitable prey, pounced upon it and carried it away. She soon found out her mistake and was in search of something eatable, when her eyes fell on the dead body of the snake lying on the Baniā's roof. She laid down the necklace on the roof and snatching the snake instead, flew away with it.

The [27]*rānī*, who had seen the kite fly away with her necklace, hastily put on her clothes, ran immediately to the king and informed him of what had happened. The king at once proclaimed it throughout the town and offered a handsome reward of Rs. 10,000 to anyone who brought back the necklace. When Somchand heard this he asked his eldest son to see if the kite had left it on his roof. "For," said he, "jewels, however costly, are of no earthly use to a kite and she is sure to have dropped it somewhere. She may have exchanged it for the snake lying on our roof."

The boy at once climbed up on the roof and with the necklace in his hands, ran down again, evidently pleased with his father's wisdom and foresight.

The Baniā took it to the king and claimed the reward which was readily granted. On his return home, he said to his children, "I hope you are now convinced of the truth of my statement that, 'Even a snake laid by has its use'".

Moral: Trifles make perfection and perfection is no trifle.

---

[27] *Rānī* = A queen.

Story 20

You are not Blind though the Spear Is

A Mahommedan named Mekhmārkhān, who lived in Dholkā, owned several acres of land that brought him in good crops; so that he had no anxiety as to his bread. From early morning till late at night he eat in the [28]*chorā*, surrounded by the idlers and gossips of the place. Thrice a day they indulged in a copious drink of opium and wine and smoked hemp and tobacco all day long.

One evening the whole set of opium-eaters went out for a walk. They were highly intoxicated and staggered as they passed along the road. Mekhmārkhān carried with him a spear, which remained perpendicular as long as the holder thereof was in his senses, but it soon assumed a horizontal position and several persons passing along the road were hurt by it; but the poor people could not raise their voice against their landlord and had to submit. A leading banker, belonging to the place, was coming from the opposite direction and he was struck by the spear. Blood began to flow copiously from the wound. The banker humbly requested the Miān either to leave his spear at home or hold it properly, to which the Moslem indignantly replied, "We landowners cannot go out without a spear or a sword; as to holding it properly, it is through your own negligence that you are hurt; for, you are not blind though the spear is."

The banker was enraged at the [29]*jāgīrdār*'s indifference and insolence. He called a meeting of the leading citizens at which

[28] *Chorā* = A public place in a vilage.

[29] *Jāgīrdār* = A landholder.

it was resolved that as it was not safe to reside in the town any longer, they should all leave it in a body.

When the *kāẓī* heard this, he went to the *jāgīrdār*, rebuked him for his misconduct and said, "you know that fine feathers make fine birds; so, when your people, on whom you depend entirely for your daily bread, have left you, what will you do and how can you manage to get on without them? You exist for your people's benefit, not they for yours, that you should use them as you please. Go to them this instant and ask their pardon for the harm you may have done them and promise never to repeat it."

Mekhmārkhān did as he was advised and the people, satisfied with his promise, returned home and lived in peace.

Moral: In the world examples of petty tyrannies, arising out of a sense of superior might, constantly abound. Might often overcome right and the weakest have to go to the wall. But

Reason and right are themselves most strong;
No kingdom got by cunning can stand long.

Story 21

I will have Her if I can; If not, what do I Lose?

A [30]*pāṭīdār* named Māthurdās, who lived in a town of Gujarat, had no children; so, both he and his wife determined to go on a pilgrimage to Ḍākore and started

[30] *Pāṭīdār* = A landholder.

in their own bullock cart. On reaching Ḍākore, they bathed in the sacred waters of the Gomatī and performed the [31]*pūjā* of [32]Śrī Ḍākore-Nātha, after receiving the impress of the shell, disc, mace and lotus — the symbols of Kṛṣṇa — on their arms, they left the place.

Half way between Ḍākore and their native town, a blind beggar was sitting by the roadside, with a rosary in his hand and uttering the name of Rāma every moment. The woman felt pity for the poor man and asked him where he was going, to which the beggar replied, [33]"*Māī*, I am blind and have lost my way. If you will kindly take me with you as far as Nāriāḍ, [34]Raṇachhoḍjī will bless you with seven children and inexhaustible riches for helping a poor blind man. The woman appealed to her husband who was anything but pleased with the physiognomy and bearing of the [35]*sādhū*. "Never trust to appearances, my dear," said the husband, "for, all that glitters is not gold. Again he is a stranger and may bring us into trouble. We had better show him the way and then leave him to himself." The *pāṭīdār* was, however, prevailed upon by the entreaties of his wife and the importunities of the beggar. They took him along with them and proceeded on their journey.

In the evening they reached Nāriāḍ where the *pāṭīdār* asked the [36]*sūrdās* to get down.

"Whom do you ask to get down?" asked *sūrdās*. "You, my

---

31 *Pūjā* = Worship.

32 Śrī Ḍākore-Nātha = The Lord of Ḍākore, i.e. Kṛṣṇa.

33 *Māī* = Mother.

34 Raṇachhoḍjī = Kṛṣṇa.

35 *Sādhū* = A religious mendicant.

36 *Sūrdās* = A blind man.

good friend," said the *pāṭīdār*, "I promised to take you as far as Nāriāḍ and here we are at its gates. We have still a long way to go and you had better make haste." To this *sūrdās* answered, "I have hired your cart for myself and my wife and now you ask us to get down before we have reached our destination! Be it so. I won't pay you a pie. Ask my wife to help me down!

"Your wife!" cried the *pāṭīdār*; "you know as well as I do that the woman sitting in the cart is my wife and not yours."

"What! You mean to rob me of her, do you?" Then addressing the woman he said, "Why don't you say something to the rogue?"

"*Sūrdās*," she replied, "you are a most ungrateful wretch and a liar besides. I did not know that you were a wolf in a sheep's clothing, or I would never have offered you a seat. Get down this moment, or we will pitch you out."

"So you are in league with the rogue, are you?" demanded *sūrdās*. "It is indeed very clever of him to have won over my wife. I shall, at once, go and ask the judge of this place to help me out of difficulty."

The *pāṭīdār* had to stop at Nāriāḍ for the night. After supper, the judge called them severally and examined them privately. The *pāṭīdār* was called upon to produce a witness who could declare on oath that they were husband and wife. This he could not do as he was quite a stranger in that part of the country. The judge, at last, hit upon a plan which he thought would bring out the fact. He ordered all the three persons to be locked in separate rooms for the night and instructed the guards to keep awake the whole night to listen attentively to what they said and to report it to him next morning.

Naturally, the *pāṭīdār* and his wife passed the whole night in loud lamentations and in reproaching themselves for having helped an undeserving wretch; while on the other hand, *sūrdās* was heard to say, "If the woman is handed over to me, so much the better. If not, what do I lose?"

The facts were duly reported to the judge, next morning, who handed over the woman to her lawful husband and sent *sūrdās* on a pilgrimage to Turaṅgābād (prison).

Moral: How often do men bring the calamities of life upon themselves and incur uncalled for liabilities on the assurances of persons whose later conduct proves them to be unworthy of confidence. Sudden trust brings sudden repentance.

If you trust before you try,
You may repent before you die ।
Cf. The Kite and Pigeons — *Aesop's Fables.*

Story 22

150 for the Beard, whereas 400 for the [37]Choṭī

In Kapadvanja there once lived a Vohorā named Ismāiljī, who, as he was returning home from his shop one dark night, was confronted by a thief, who caught hold of the Vohorā's beard and would not let it go unless and until he paid Rs. 150. This happened just in front of the Vohorā's house. As

---

[37] *Choṭī* or *choṭalī* = Hair on the middle of head.

if he were addressing his wife, the Mullāh exclaimed "Do you hear! The thief here demands 150 rupees as the price of my beard. Bring the money here at once, for, if he lets it go and catches hold of the *choṭī*, which is of greater importance and consequently of greater value and then demands 400 rupees for it, we shall have to pay it! Why not then pay 150 and make a saving of 250?" The greedy thief released his hold on the beard and at once made for the hair on the head, for he knew not that the Vohorās as a class do not wear *choṭī*.

This presence of mind stood the Vohorā in good stead; for, as soon as he found himself free, he ran into his house and shut the door against the unwelcome visitor who went away bemoaning his own folly and covetousness.

Moral: Catch not at the shadow and lose the substance. The story contains a caution against excessive greed which oftentime misses what it aims at.

Cf. "The Dog and the Shadow" — *Aesop's Fables.*

Story 23

Plate this Club with Gold!

A beggar was begging alms in the *bāẓār*, with a thick club in his hand. Passing from shop to shop, he arrived at a goldsmith's who was hammering a piece of gold into leaf. The tempting yellow metal attracted the beggar's eye and no wonder; for, nothing can withstand the power of gold. He was a beggar by profession and avarice had blinded his eyes. Without considering, therefore, the reasonableness or otherwise of the demand, he asked the goldsmith to plate his club with gold! The goldsmith looked up and stared at the beggar, for some time, in surprise, at which the latter exclaimed, "Well my boy, don't you hear me? Plate this club with gold and God will bless you." "Gold is not to be had for asking", said the goldsmith. "You seem to have lost your head or you would not make such an unreasonable demand." "Asking for it has cost me nothing; had you met my demand, you would have been the loser and not I!" so saying he left the place.

Moral: Gold is the dust that blinds all eyes.

Story 24

No, by My Grandfather, I am not Hungry

A countryman once visited the city of Ahmedabad and put up with a distant relative of his who lived there. The prosperous citizen set before his country guest a good supply of delicious food and pressed him to do full justice to it. After dinner he served him with *pān-supārī* as dessert. The villager, thinking it to be another dish, said, "I have had enough food. I won't take any more." "It will help digestion," said his host, "and do you good." "But I tell you I am not hungry. You have not eaten much, so you might take it."

Hospitality forbids me to taste it unless you take some.

"By my grandfather," exclaimed the visitor, "I am not

hungry. If I were, I wouldn't have left that leaf" – meaning the plantain leaf on which the food was served!

Out of regard to the feelings of his ignorant guest, the host refrained from explaining to him that *pān-supārī* was no food, but a sort of dessert to be taken after each meal.

Story 25

I Give You All the Buffaloes of the Town

A company of itinerant actors were once playing in a street of Dhraṅgadharā. After going through several performances, they brought in a dancer who played his part exquisitely and faultlessly. Gifts began to pour in from the audience. A Baniā named Lapoddās, who was greatly charmed with the performance, offered a buffalo in a moment of excitement; but the next instant he was sorry for what he had done and wished to recall the offer if he could do so by any means.

Next came two actors in the characters of an ill-assorted couple. Seizing the opportunity, the Baniā, as though greatly pleased, offered two buffaloes more. A little later he offered ten. Towards the end of the play, he got up from his seat and cried out, "I give you all the buffaloes of the town!"

The bystanders and the actors thought the Baniā had lost his senses, or he would not have made such an absurd offer; for, he had no right to give away the buffaloes belonging to other people. By feigning insanity, the Baniā thus easily recalled the original offer and congratulated himself on his ingenuity.

Moral: A promise breaker is never at a loss for an evasion.

Story 26

Law Licks up All

A Bania named Oghaḍ once lived in a village of Kāṭhiāwāṛ. In the same compound stood the house of another Baniā Rāmā. Both had a common claim on the unbuilt land constituting the compound. With the intention of adding a room to his house, Oghaḍ measured the space between the two houses and drove a peg therein.

Rāmā, instead of proceeding to a law court, went before the [38]*mahājana* and lodged a complaint against his neighbour. The *mahājana* went with him, examined the land under dispute and were satisfied as to the justice of Rāmā's complaint. They summoned Oghaḍ and asked him to remove the peg from the land that was their common property. To this request, Oghaḍ replied, "The land belongs to me and I am therefore justified in doing what I will with it. "It does not belong to you alone", was the reply of the *mahājana*; "you can't misappropriate it with impunity. If Rāmā goes to law, it will go hard with you." "Who says I have misappropriated it?" Demanded Oghaḍ.

"We say so"; responded the *mahājana*. "Remember that the voice of the people is the voice of God. It is for your own good that we ask you to remove the peg."

---

[38] *Mahājana* = Leading persons of the Baniā community.

"Ah! I know that very well and am thankful to you for your excellent advice"; sneered Oghaḍ. "But the peg is where it ought to be and I am not going to take it out."

"You obstinate brute," replied the *mahājana*, "if you won't listen to us now, it will be too late to grieve when that chance is past."

"*Mahājana* are my [39]*mā-bāp*, but I am sorry I can't remove the peg for them"; was the final answer of Oghaḍ.

The *mahājana* did all they could to dissuade Oghaḍ from doing an injustice to his neighbour, but when they found that nothing would make him change his mind, they advised the aggrieved party to file a suit against him in a law-court.

Rāmā did as he was advised and he summoned the *mahājana* as witnesses who declared on oath that the land in question was common property. The judge ordered Oghaḍ to remove the peg at once and pay the expenses of the suit. Moreover, Oghaḍ had to engage pleaders and shut up his shop for several days, which entailed a heavy drain upon his small resources. He came to his senses at last, but not till all was consumed and repentance was too late.

Moral: Avoid law-suits above all things; they affect your conscience, impair your health and dissipate your property.

"Fools and obstinste persons enrich the lawyers", says an Italian Proverb.

---

[39] *Mā-bāp* = Parents.

Story 27

Something, if You could but Tell What

Once upon a time, the Emperor Akbar asked his favourite jester Lahūwā which was the most prudent and circumspect community, to which Lahūwā replied that the Baniās were.

"Nonsense!" said Akbar. "They are most clumsy fellows." "They look clumsy, no doubt; but all the same, they are very thoughtful"; responded Lahūwā. Whereupon the emperor ordered him to prove it to him.

Lahūwā at once ordered a maund of [40]*mag* from the royal granary and summoning a few Baniās from the bazaar, he asked them what it was. The Baniās thought to themselves that it must be out of policy or for some secret purpose that the question was asked. They resolved, therefore, not to name the thing and when questioned again by Lahūwā, one of them said, "It is a sort of food grain". "You are quite right", said another Baniā. "Besides when we pound it into meal and take off the husks, it tastes delicious!" "Quite so!" assented a third Baniā. "I like it very much."

"But what do you call it?" demanded the emperor.

"Is n't it [41]*adad?*" asked one Baniā to another. "No"; replied his companion. "*Adad* is black whereas this is green." "It can't be pepper either," added the third; "for, that is also black."

At this the emperor became very angry and losing patience, he exclaimed, "you are a pack of idiots. Don't you see it is *mag?*"

---

40 *Mag* = A kind of pulse.

41 *Adad* = A kind of pulse.

"So it is!" cried out the Baniās simultaneously. "The name had escaped our memories."

Lahūwā, then asked them to repeat the name to which the sly Baniās replied, "His Majesty is quite right. We too call it by the same name." Then turning to the emperor they asked, "What do you call it, Your Majesty?"

The emperor was convinced that if not wise, the Baniās were at least the most circumspect community he had ever seen.

Story 28

A Sequel to the Above

But after this the Emperor Akbar wished to take in the Baniās by some means or other and he asked Lahūwā to show him a trick by which he could do so. The jester advised him to go a hunting, kill a wild boar, drag it to the gates of Delhi, hang it there and then ask the Baniās what it was. If they said, "[42]A boar, your Majesty" they were liable to be punished for abusing their sovereign.

Next day, the emperor did as Lahūwā had suggested and summoning the leaders of the Baniā community he asked them what the animal was. The Baniās at once perceived that it was a trick of Lahūwā's to entrap them. They resolved therefore, to refrain from calling the beast by its proper name and to try the emperor's patience by beating about the bush. When,

[42] A boar, Your Majesty = Means in Gujarati "Your Majesty is a boar".

therefore, asked again by the emperor, one of them said, “It looks like an elephant kept without food and water for a long time and consequently much reduced!” A second Baniā after consideration replied, “It is too small for an elephant. I think it is a large wild cat!” “Don’t you see it has a tusk, while cats have none?” Said another. “It is a rhinoceros, without doubt!”

This was too much for the emperor. He seized one of the Baniās by the collar and pointing to the boar, he angrily exclaimed, “Look at it again, you blind fellows and tell me; is n’t it a wild boar?” “It is! so it is!” cried out the wise sons of silly mothers.

Moral: It is wise to consider a course of conduct in all its bearings, before we determine on it. Before venturing out an opinion, we should weigh well the consequences. This story as well as the preceding one teaches as prudence, patience and foresight.

Story 29

The Dog of Hadālā

Hadālā is a small village situated on the borders of the Bhāl, a fresh water Runn, in a country without hills or forests and almost a level plain. There lived outside the village a dog who was in the habit of barking at every passerby, whenever she caught sight of one till he disappeared from view. This meant a good deal in a level country and she had to attend to her unpleasant duty from early morning till late at night. This process of barking all day long had strengthened her jaws and made her proof against cold, heat and fatigue. The villagers knew her nature and often teased her which gave them great amusement.

Before the establishment of the British rule, the tributary chiefs of Kāṭhiāwāṛ paid tribute to the Gāekwāṛ of Barodā, but not as regularly and readily as they do now. The Gāekwāṛ had to send troops on the [43]Mulakgiri expedition. Once such a punitive force, on its way to a native state, passed by Hadālā and the indefatigable dog took to her profession at sight of the strangers. The sepoys were seen marching on the plain of Bhāl from early morning to late in the afternoon. It would have tried the patience of a caravan dog, but this untiring and energetic bow-wow of Hadālā was quite equal to the occasion and kept on howling all the while. In the evening, however, she felt so tired and exhausted that she dropped senseless on the ground and fits of convulsions put an end to her existence, at which the villagers exclaimed, "Die as you deserve".

Moral: Our misfortunes are often brought on us by ourselves. So blind are we that only too frequently we wing the arrow which is to pierce our own heart.

43 Mulakgiri expedition = Expedition for the collection of tribute.

Story 30

Tidings of the Well-being of the Ṭhākore's Family

During the disastrous famine of 1934 AV (1878 CE), a [44]Ṭhākore left his native village and went to a distant part of Gujarat to earn his bread. During his absence, his house and haystacks were burnt to ashes and all the members of his family died of diseases and starvation. Not a pennyworth of his once handsome property, not a single soul of his once extensive family, remained, except an old servant who set out in search of his young master, to convey to him the sad news of his bereavement.

After wandering from place to place for a long time, he at last fell in with the Ṭhākore who embraced him with tears of joy in his eyes and inquired after the health of his dear ones. The faithful servant thought that if he revealed the sad tidings all at once, it would break his master's heart. He, therefore, resolved to break it as gently as possible.

"Well, my friend," began the Ṭhākore, "are all at home doing well?"

"All, except our poor dog Bāziā."

"It grieves me very much to hear that my poor old dog is no more. Of what did he die?"

"Our mare Hardi died," replied the servant. "The dog ate her flesh and followed her to the grave."

---

[44] Ṭhākore = A landholder.

"What happened to my dear mare? I am very sorry to have lost both my pets."

"She died for want of hay and gram."

"When I left home, there was a large stock of both. Where did it all go?"

"A part of it was destroyed by fire and the remainder was disposed of in order to defray the expenses of feeding the Brahmin on the 13th day after your mother's death." Shocked at this last blow the Ṭhākore exclaimed, "My mother! Is she also no more? Of what did she die?"

"The loss of your only son told heavily upon her health and she succumbed to the blow."

This utterly overwhelmed the Thakore. "My son! My only son! Oh! My God!" he cried. "I don't know what to believe and what not to believe. What happened to my darling?"

"He died for want of proper nourishment." Do you mean to say that my wife did not nourish her own child? "That is absurd!"

"She did suckle him and took great care of him as long as she was alive; but after her decease, the tender child was too helpless to live without a mother's care."

"So my wife is also dead!" sobbed the Ṭhākore. "Whom have I left then in the world? Let us go home where I can lay myself down in a quiet corner and weep over my misfortunes."

"Even that last consolation is denied you"; replied the servant sadly. "Before I left, a great fire broke out in the vicinity of our house and utterly destroyed it together with other houses."

The Ṭhākore gave up the idea of returning home and finished his miserable life abroad.

Story 31

To Do as Bhagā Did

There formerly lived in Kairā a Baniā named Bhagwāndās whom everybody called Bhagā, a contracted form of his long name. His father died when Bhagā was only a child and so, being the only child of a widowed mother, he was never sent to school and was spoilt through fondness and indulgence. Besides, he was married at the early age of 12 and had never stirred out from home till he was twenty years of age. It then happened that Bhagā and his wife were invited by his father-in-law to be present on the occasion of a marriage. His wife was too ill to go, so it was decided that Bhagā should go alone When he came to take leave of his mother, she said, "My boy, you are still a child and ignorant of the ways of the world. I am very sorry to have to send you, but it can't be helped. Conduct yourself well and speak as little as possible when you are once there. Don't utter two words where you can do with one and be careful to avoid long explanations where you can manage equally well with the monosyllables "yes and no".

Bhagā made up his mind to follow the advice of his mother to the very letter and say "yes and no" by turns to every question that might be asked. In the evening of the same day he reached his father-in-law's house where he was heartily welcomed. His mother-in-law performed the benedictory ceremony, after which the following dialogue took place between them.

"Have you come by yourself?" Began his mother-in-law. "Yes."

"Hasn't my daughter accompanied you?"

"No."

"Is your mother doing well?" "Yes."

"Are all your people quite well?" "No."

"Is my daughter still ill?" "Yes."

"Doesn't she feel any better?" "No."

Much alarmed, Bhagā's mother-in-law eagerly asked, "Have you placed her under the treatment of a competent physician?" "Yes."

"Does he give any hopes?" "No."

In great distress the poor woman said, "I hope there wasn't anything very serious when you left! was there?"

Bhagā who was greatly bored by this series of questions put on a gloomy face and replied, "Yes!" "Why did you not write to us then?" Eagerly exclaimed the mother-in-law. "I hope she is still alive Is she?"

Bhagā who thought that the cross-examination would never come to an end, replied with a dejected look, "No!"

"Is my daughter dead then?" Asked the woman with tears in her eyes: "Yes" replied Bhagā.

This was followed by loud lamentations, when Bhagā's father-in-law accompanied by a guest from Kairā came into find his wife and daughters beating their breasts and weeping piteously. On inquiry, he was told that his eldest daughter that is Bhagā's wife was dead! The newcomer who had seen her alive just before he left Kairā, interposed, "Who says she is dead? I saw her only this morning and that too not in a very bad state of health."

"My son-in-law here says that she is dead!" said the mother-in-law. Bhagā was further examined and the truth came out at last!

The ignorance and thoughtlessness of Bhagā have become proverbial, so that anybody who does a foolish thing has the nickname of Bhagā bestowed upon him and he is said to have done as Bhagā did.

Story 32

Fool's Haste is no Speed

In Bhāvnagar there once lived a Baniā named Kamalshi who had a servant named Hiro a stupid boy, who was therefore only employed in running errands for his master.

Having some business at Ghoghā (Gogo) Kamalshi thought of despatching Hiro the next morning. The silly boy, who was informed of his master's intention by one of his fellow-servants, thought to himself, [45]"Śeṭh calls me a fool. This is an excellent opportunity of showing him that I am not so stupid as he supposes. If, in this case, I act in anticipation of his orders, it will open his eyes and convince him that I am no fool!"

[45] Śeṭh = Master.

Next morning, he got up very early and left for Ghoghā, whence he returned in the evening. With high hopes of his services being properly appreciated he ran to his master and said, "Śeṭh Sāheb, I come directly from Ghoghā where I went this morning!" "Who asked you to go there and for what?" asked the master. "Why," said Hiro, "I was told that you thought of sending me there this morning and I have anticipated your wishes! as to business, I was told nothing or I would have done it!"

The master laughed at his folly and dismissed him with instructions never to repeat it.

Moral: Persons of Hiro's type are not rare in this world. They over-rate their abilities and expose themselves to the ridicule of others.

Story 33

[46]Ḍheḍas as Arbitrators

Once in a Native State, the post of [47]*kārbhārī* fell vacant. From among a number of applications, one was selected and the candidate was summoned for a personal interview.

The native states of India are generally hot beds of intrigue and party spirit and the *kārbhārī* is safe only as long as he has a stronghold over the *rājā* and his hangers on. This never lasts long and one *kārbhārī* has to make way for another in quick

[46] Ḍheḍas = Scavangers.

[47] *Kārbhārī* = Minister.

succession. None knows this better than a *kārbhārī* and he takes up the appointment with a view to collect as much money as he possibly can, by fair means or foul, during his short tenure of office. If, however, he is not a match for the wire-pullers, he is not allowed to depart in peace and has to pay a heavy fine when he leaves office.

The newcomer, who had served half a dozen states in the course of a decade, expressed his willingness to take up the responsible post, on condition that if ever he fell into disgrace, he should not be fined by the king.

"If you commit a fault," replied the *rājā*, "you are liable to punishment; and who can punish the first officer of my state but myself?" "But in that case," replied the *kārbhārī*, "we become partisans and one party cannot impartially deal with the fault of the other. I wish, therefore, that I may be tried by arbitrators." "And whom would you suggest as arbitrators?" Demanded the king.

"The Ḍheḍas! men of the lowest caste!" announced the *kārbhārī*. "They are neither my relatives nor connected with me in any way and capable, therefore, of deciding my case impartially."

Greatly astonished, the king said, "Ḍheḍas sit in judgement upon my officer! that is ridiculous! you don't mean that! do you? "I do, my lord. I would rather be tried by Ḍheḍas than expose myself to the tender mercies of my brother officers and self-styled friends! I am prepared to accept the post only on that condition."

The king granted his request, bestowed upon him a dress of honour and installed him on the [48]*dīwān*'s *gaddī*.

---

[48] *Dīwān's gaddī* = Minister's seat.

No sooner was the new *kārbhārī* established in his office, than he began to devise means – fair and foul – to extract the maximum of riches in the minimum of time. A number of unjust taxes were imposed upon the people and justice was sold to the highest bidder.

The people at last grew so tired of the oppressive measures put in force by the new minister, that they submitted a petition to the king representing all their grievances. The anti-*kārbhārī* party, availing themselves of the opportunity induced the king to try the minister for mis-appropriation of public money.

The king at once summoned the *kārbhārī* and angrily exclaimed, "Many charges against you have come to my knowledge and I don't see why you should not be fined first and then dismissed!"

"If I have fallen into disgrace," answered the minister, "I don't wish to serve any longer; as regards the trial, I must be tried by Ḍheḍas as was agreed upon."

The king called the leaders of the Ḍheḍa community and instructed them to impartially conduct the trial without the least fear, as the *kārbhārī* was no longer in power and could therefore do them no harm. The Ḍheḍas then arranged themselves in a circle under a *nīm*-tree standing in front of the palace and began to consider what fine to impose upon the *kārbhārī*.

"Brethren," said a leading Ḍheḍa, "the case is a serious one and cannot, therefore, be disposed of off hand."

"The wily *kārbhārī* has made quite a fortune", remarked another. "Of how much do you think he has robbed the state and the people?"

"Not less than five score of rupees, I am sure!" said a third. "But we will make him refund the whole sum!"

"That's too heavy a fine, I think"; replied the first speaker. "We should not be too strict. Let us impose a fine of two score and a half!"

This was unanimously agreed upon and the *kārbhārī* was right glad to escape with so slight a punishment.

Moral: A prince wants a million, a beggar a groat.

Story 34

It is a [49]Miā's Field, not a Widow's

When the province of Gujarat was under the Mahommeden rule, two horsemen left Ahmedabad, one day, for a neighbouring village. Both of them were shabbily dressed and their horses looked half starved. At that time there were no roads, so they had to pass through fields and forests. After travelling for some time, they came to a field in which was standing a *bājarī*-crop of excellent growth. At the sight of the green field, the riders dismounted and let loose their horses to feed upon the *bājarī*. Before they could do any damage, however, their eyes fell on the owner of the field coming towards them from the other side of the field, stick in hand. At the sight of him, the sepoys remounted their horses and hurriedly left the place.

---

[49] Miā = A Mahommedan.

A little further on, they came upon another field which belonged to an old Brahmin widow. The Mahommedans leisurely got down from their horses and let them loose in the field which was not their own. When the poor widow saw the horses trampling the tender crop under their feet and doing a lot of harm she came before their owners and with folded arms exclaimed, "I am a helpless widow and solely dependent upon the crop of this field. God will bless you, if you leave it unmolested."

The sepoys instead of listening to her entreaties, mounted their horses and rode right across the field trampling down the stalks and ears of corn that came in their way.

Adjoining the widow's field there was another field belonging to a Mahommedan. The horsemen thought that that too belonged to the widow, so they entered it fearlessly. When the owner of the field saw them, he came running towards them accompanied by three or four labourers. Without uttering a word, they pulled them down and beat them severely. When they had chastized them to their hearts content, the owner of the field ordered them to remount the horses. When they had done so, he said, "You ought to have known that this was a Miā's field and not a widow's".

The horsemen meekly left the place. The Miā had taught them a lesson which lasted them their lifetime and they never again entered a field that belonged to a Mahommedan.

Moral: In this world superior might generally prevails and the weakest have to go to the wall.

Story 35

Putting One off does not Necessarily Imply Refusal

A Mussalman was in the habit of buying everything on credit and putting off the payment from day-to-day. Thus he had lost his credit and nobody advanced him anything except on cash payment. He owed some money to a Baniā who pressed him everyday for payment.

Once when the Miā was in a cheerful frame of mind, the Baniā asked him to settle the long-standing account. The debt was settled at 60 rupees and 40 rupees were added as interest, making up a total of 100 rupees. The Miā showed his unwillingness to pay the interest which he declared unlawful according to the tenets of [50]Islam and asked the creditor to take off a part of the principal also; to this the Baniā replied, "Business is business, my friend. In account matters we count like jews and agree like brothers. Trade knows neither friends nor kindred."

The Miā got wild and angrily exclaimed, "The interest is out of question, for, my religious principles forbid me to pay or receive it; that leaves sixty; you must forego half that sum; out of the remaining thirty, I shall pay you ten in a day or two, another ten will be paid later on and for the remaining don't bother yourself about it!"

Thus the Miā disposed of the account without paying a pie!

[50] Islam = The Mahommedan religion.

Story 36

Good Head is Better than a Hundred Strong Hands

Once upon a time, a king was hunting in a forest, when a hare was started from her form. The king followed her leaving his attendants far behind. At last, heat and fatigue overcame him and he laid himself down under a banyan tree.

Two [51]Kunbī boys happened to pass by the tree. The king asked them to procure him some food and water, which they did. When he had allayed his hunger and thirst, he asked the boys to demand anything they liked and it should be granted. One of the two thought to himself, "I haven't got a cow or a buffalo at home. If, therefore, I ask for one, the king will be sure to give it to me and I shall be ever so happy." He therefore prayed the king to bestow upon him a stout buffalo, a request which was readily granted.

The other Kunbī, who was a lad of fifteen said to himself, "I am not going to have a cow or a buffalo; for, it's no permanent good. Even if he grants me a [52]*jāgīr* and raises me to the rank of a [53]*jāgīrdār*, I won't accept it; for, I am illiterate and cannot manage it. [54]Lakṣmī is restless and volatile, while her sister [55]Saravatī is steady and reliable. I would rather have her than her fickle sister; because, wealth is worth little without wisdom and it is skill and wisdom and not wealth and riches, that govern

---

51 Kunbī = A class of cultivators.

52 *Jāgīr* = Landed property.

53 *Jāgīrdār* = A landed proprietor.

54 Lakṣmī = The Godess of riches.

55 Sarasvatī = The Godess of learning.

the world. I would rather have a grain of sense than a pound of gold." When asked, therefore, by the king, what he wanted, he thoughtfully replied, "May it please your Majesty, I would rather have a liberal education bestowed upon me, than the most costly things of this world; for, learning is an acquisition that can neither be stolen by thieves, burnt by fire, nor divided among brothers."

The king took them both with him to his capital, and on reaching the royal palace he at once ordered a buffalo to be given to the lad who had asked for it. He then summoned a [56]*paṇḍit* and entrusted the other boy to his care, with instructions to teach him with great care and promptitude.

The lad with the buffalo was made much of and praised for his practical wisdom by the villagers, while the younger boy was made fun of and laughed at, for having preferred learning to a buffalo which yielded 10 seers of milk every day.

But the boy entrusted to the *paṇḍit* showed great capacity and made amazing progress in all the branches of Sanskrit literature. In five years he had learnt everything that was worth learning and had the responsible post of a Revenue Commissioner bestowed upon him. The king was so pleased with his work that he conferred upon him a handsome *jāgīr* and raised him to the rank of a *jāgīrdār*. Thus he made a fortune and did a lot of good to other people, while the man with the buffalo remained in the same abject condition and finished his days in obscurity. Ere long he discovered his mistake and was often heard to say, "One good head is better than a hundred strong hands".

---

[56] *Paṇḍit* = A religious preceptor.

Story 37

There is no Going Back

A Mahommedan went to a Baniā's shop and asked the rates of flour, *ghee*, sugar, pulse and rice. After much higgling they came to terms and the prices agreed upon were much lower than the market rates of those articles. The Miā thought all the while that he had secured very low rates, while the Baniā thought of recovering by false weights what he had lost by the reduced rates.

When the things were weighed and handed over to the Miā, he suspected some fraud, for the articles he bought, looked less in bulk than those he usually obtained from another grocer. Without speaking a word, he seized the scales with which the things were weighed but on examination they were found to be correct. Then he caught hold of the weights and asked the Baniā to accompany him to the nearest police-station to get them verified. The Baniā knew quite well that the weights were false and that he would be severely punished for cheating. He, therefore, offered to re-weigh the things by a correct set of weights and thus make good the loss; but the Miā would not let him go unpunished.

The Baniā then appealed to his neighbours who begged the Miā to let him go for this once, but the Mussalman was so enraged that he began to abuse all who came near him. Seeing that entreaties would avail nothing, several Baniās put a five-pound weight in a gunny bag and attacked the Mahommedan from all sides. When they had struck him hard and deprived him of the weights in his possession they let him go to do what he liked. The Miā complained against them all in a law-court but he could not prove the charge, for the place where he was beaten was all inhabited by Baniās and none therefore came forward to corroborate his statement. Again there were no perceptible marks on his body to prove the assault.

This story has given rise to the following proverb:

"Tease not a Mahommedan in [57]*kasbā*; play not with fire in summer; don't find fault with a robber in the forest; or a Baniā in the bazaar".

Story 38

Foolish Boasting

There lived in Delhi a Mahommedan and a Rājpūt named Fakkaḍ Khān and Randhīrsinh respectively. They were great friends and passed much of their time in each other's company. Once when they were sitting together and talking about the golden past, Fakkaḍ said, "Times are altered. My father was a [58]*risāldar* in the Imperial cavalry. There were so many horses in his stable that it took days to count them all! and the stable! one end of it was in the extreme north and other reached the extreme south!"

The Rājpūt, in order to show his friend that it was a cock and bull story, put on a serious look and said, "you are quite right friend. My father was as fond of swords and lances as was your

57 *Kasbā* = A street chiefly inhabited by Mahommedans.

58 *Risāldār* = A Commanding Officer in a cavalry.

father of fine horses. He had a lance, one end of which touched the earth and the other reached the sky!"

"That can't be. Where, on earth, did he keep it?" asked the Miā.

"In your father's stable." replied the Rājpūt.

Moral: Foolish boasting exposes us to merited ridicule.

Cf. "The fox and the Crocodile" — *Aesop's Fables.*

Story 39

No Shift and One Too Many

A hare, a snake and a fox were friends and lived together in a haystack. One night it caught fire and the three friends began to look for a safe means of escape. "Don't trouble about me"; said the hare. "I have a hundred tricks to resort to." So saying she entered her form which was underneath the haystack. "Be easy on my account"; said the snake. "For I have a thousand and one ways of escape. I can enter the bowels of the earth like our friend the hare, as well as I can climb a tree. A tree would be the best resort under the circumstances. So saying he climbed a tree that overhung the haystack. The fox who had but one shift — that of running away from the proximity of danger — made good her escape in the woods.

The haystack was soon reduced to ashes. The poor hare, who had sought refuge under it, was baked alive and the flames rose so high that the tree, in which the snake had sought protection, was blackened and the foolish reptile perished with it. Reynard alone escaped unhurt.

Moral: Evil awaits him that has no shift and him that has too many. The man with many expedients generally fails. He begins many plans and finishes none.

Cf. The Cat and the Fox. — *Aesop's Fables.*

Story 40

Rejecting a Bribe of A Hundred Thousand Rupees! (A true story)

Ambashanker, a native of Sūrat and a member of the Brahmakshatri caste, has gained a great reputation for upright conduct. The following is one of the numerous instances of his honesty and truthful dealing.

Once, during his tenure of a Magistrate's office in Ahmedabad, there arose a complicated question of legacy in a millionaire Pārekh family. The case came before Ambashanker. With the object of winning over the Magistrate to his side, one of the parties went one night to Ambashanker and offered him the sum of 100,000 rupees, if he decided the case in his favour. This handsome offer of 62 maunds of silver or 125 lbs of gold would have blinded any other man, but Ambashanker had too high an ideal of justice and honesty to be tempted by gold or silver. He, therefore, disdainfully rejected the bribe and asked the man to go away.

"Why are you angry?" said the man. "The service of your whole life will not bring you as much money as I mean to place in your hands to night. Seize the opportunity, my dear Sir and take advantage of the smiles of fortune. Again, your secret will be safe with me and nobody will ever know it. Fortune knocks at your door and if you don't let her in, she will pass away."

"Parekh," said the Magistrate, "I thank you for your advice and would certainly have followed it; but I am not my own master, for I am responsible to the higher tribunal of duty presided over by Justice Conscience! Who is very keen about such matters and cannot put up with the slightest infringement of the principles laid down by him. You say that nobody would refuse such a handsome offer, but there are persons who consider duty above all things. You will, therefore, do well to leave me alone."

Story 41

To Strain at a Gnat and Swallow a Camel

There lived in Calcutta a Mahommedan named Nekī-khān, who, notwithstanding his extreme poverty, had established a reputation as an honest man. Whenever he found a thing lying on the road or elsewhere, he invariably returned it to its owner and never asked for [59]*cheri-meri* from him.

One day, as Nekī-khān was passing through a street, his eyes

[59] *Cheri-meri* = Small presents.

fell on a small parcel and a [60]*kauṛī* lying in the middle of the road. He picked them up and went home directly. On opening the parcel, a priceless treasure consisting of a pearl necklace and a pair of gold bangles, set with diamonds, met his eyes. His first impulse was to find out their lawful owner and hand them over to him, but on second thoughts, he came to the conclusion that he would appropriate them for himself. Pitying my poor condition and helpless old age, God may have sent it to me as a reward. Again, I am getting old and shall have to retire from service in a year or two, so this will serve as a provision against rainy days to come. "Spontaneous bounty", says Gorakhnāth, "is like milk, that which is begged is like water and that which is snatched away is like blood." I have neither begged nor stolen it. It is a God-send and as such is most acceptable. This false reasoning could not, however, silence the voice of conscience. "I have enjoyed an unsullied reputation so long"; said he to himself; "Why tarnish it now in the eve of my life and disgrace my white hair? But then; when fortune knocks at my door, it is foolish to turn her away. Honesty is the best policy, no doubt, but it is often left to starve."

He was thus at a loss to come to a decision one way or the other when an idea struck him. He at once went out with the parcel and the *kauṛī* and passing from street to street he cried out in a very loud tone, "Has anyone lost a *kauṛī*?" adding in voice that was scarcely audible, "and a parcel of ornaments?" No claimant was found, for, who would care to recover a *kauṛī* even if he had lost one? Having thus satisfied his conscience he returned home in the evening and quietly buried the parcel in a safe corner of his house?

60 *Kauṛī* = A shell.

Moral: The attempt of the dishonest Miā is a true image of men who act as if they thought God could not read the secrets of their hearts and think to deceive the All-seeing and All-wise.

Cf. "Smooth dissimulation! Skilled to grace"; "A devil's purpose with an angel's face".

Story 42

All Saint Without, All Devil Within

There was a [61]Kolī named Bhalo who pretended to be vary pious and devout. Carrying a rosary of beads in one hand, in the other in country guitar and with a mark made with the sacred yellow earth upon his forehead, he chanted hymns day and night in praise of Rāma. He preached broad principles of morality to the villagers and exhorted them to be honest, truthful and god-fearing. All this, however, was meant for the market, not for home consumption. In short, he was fair without, but foul within.

Once a body of pilgrims was going to Kāśī (modern Benares) and Bhalo Bhagat accompanied them. After bathing in the sacred waters of the mother Ganges, they performed their obeisance to the Lord of Kāśī and took certain vows. Bhalo took a vow never to go fishing.

On his way back, he came upon a pool of water, about a mile from his native place, abounding in fish. He had a great wish to take some, but he could not do so, as he had taken a vow to

[61] Kolī = A member of the labouring class.

that effect. At last he hit upon a plan that would answer his purpose without violating the vow. From the pool to the village gate, he traced a line with his stick and when his caste-fellows came to welcome him home, he uttered the following words which if rightly interpreted would lead them to the pool: "I will neither point it out with my finger, nor utter a word as to its whereabout; but if you follow the track of the stick, it will guide you to a pool of plenty!"

Two or three Kolīs at once made for the pool and on arriving there, caught a number of fish and brought them home to be served to the [62]*Bhagat.* Thus the so-called *Bhagat* got the fish and kept his vow as well.

Moral:

"Oh! what a man may within him hide",
"Though angel on the outward side".

Cf. also: "Words and promises that yoke"; "The 'utterer' are quickly broke"; "Like Samson's Cuffs, though by his own"; "Direction and advice put on".

Story 43

He That is Won with a Nut may be Lost with An Apple

In one of the native states under the Rewā Kāṇṭhā Agency, there was a Magistrate named Anādidās who sold justice to the highest bidder firmly believing that gold is the god

62 *Bhagat* = A religious man.

of the world. He never looked to the merits or demerits of the case, or considered pros and cons, but decided it in favour of the party who offered the highest price for a decision in his favour.

A widow of the Khavās community owed 250 rupees to a Baniā who filed a suit against her in Anāndidās's court. The Baniā who knew the Magistrate well, bought a turban worth Rs. 30 and presented it to him, on condition that a decree should be passed in his favour. The Magistrate, while accepting the turban, assured the Baniā that it would surely be decided in his favour.

When the case came before the court for hearing, the Magistrate showed a marked tendency towards the Baniā, which led the shrewd widow to suspect some foul play. She, therefore, prayed the court for an adjournment which was readily granted.

The same evening she went to the Magistrate's house and after talking for some time on indifferent topics, she said, "you don't seem to have a cow or a buffalo. Take my advice and keep one. But then cattle are so scarce nowadays. Never mind. I have a good, strong buffalo that gives twenty pounds of milk a day and as I am a lonely widow, I have no use for it. I will send it to you tomorrow morning, if you will but accept it." The greedy judge readily gave his consent and asked the woman if he could do anything for her. "You know," replied the woman, "that a Baniā has filed a suit against me, which is to come before you next Monday. I am a poor widow and cannot afford to pay such a large sum. If you, therefore, dismiss the suit and help me out, I shall owe you a lifelong debt of gratitude."

On the fixed day, the Magistrate took up the case. After examining the Baniā's account-books, he said, "You seem to have deceived this poor widow who knows very little of matters of account." The Baniā at once understood the cause of this sudden change in the Magistrate's conduct and in order to remind him of the turban he said, "What about the turban, Sir!" "The turban has been swallowed up by the buffalo, my friend!" replied the Magistrate coolly. He then dismissed the suit.

Moral: Judges should be disinterested.

Cf. "The dog and the sheep". — *Aesop's Fables.*

Story 44

A Fig to the Doctor when Cured

There lived in Daman a merchant named Boghāśā who lost so heavily in a business transaction that he was unable to meet the demands of his numerous creditors. He, therefore, shut up his shop and kept indoors to escape the various demands for payment. A friend of his named Dhirajlal, knowing that Boghāśā was in great trouble went to his house and asked him how the matter stood.

"My friend," said Boghāśā, "you know that I have incurred a very heavy loss in that wheat transaction. As a banker of long-standing and some reputation, I hold deposits from a number of persons; I am quite unable to satisfy them all at the present moment. If you can show me a way out of it, you will lay me under a life-long obligation."

"You know as well as I do," replied Dhirajlal, "that you owe me to a large sum. Now if I show you a nice trick to get out of the difficulty, promise me that you won't put it in force against me also."

"You need not be afraid of that; for, I am not so ungrateful as that. Once I am free from the clutches of my other creditors I will pay up every pie that I owe you."

"Listen to me then," said Dhirajlal, "whenever a creditor comes and asks you for payment, say 'mew' in reply to every question that is asked you. They would then think that sudden misfortune has affected your brains. You will thus be left unmolested and in the end you will come off successful! But mind, the policy of 'A fig to the doctor when cured' won't do for me!"

From early morning next day, creditors began to pour in, but Boghāśā met them all with that excellent monosyllable "mew".

"Settle my account, Boghāśā" cried a Baniā.

"Mew!" replied the debtor.

"That won't do"; shouted a banker. "Pay me this instant, or I will take legal steps against you."

"Mew" was Boghāśā's only reply to the threat.

"I have deposited a hundred rupees with you. I want them back this moment"; cried a woodcutter.

"Mew!"

Then a widow spoke, "Śeṭh Sāheb, you know that I am solely dependent on the interest that my deposit brings me every month. The loss of it would render me utterly helpless; I have no other means of livelihood. You must pay me, if you can't pay the others."

"Mew!"

"Some do the sowing and others do the reaping", grumbled a cultivator. "That's not fair. You will have to repay what you have received from us."

"Mew!"

"Why do you make a pain of a pleasure?" suggested a [63]*vaidya*. "Make a part payment only, if you can't pay up the whole and we will be satisfied."

"Mew!"

The creditors, at last got tired and thought the game was not worth the candle. So, they gave up the attempt and went home. The remedy proved very efficacious and Boghāśā stuck to it with great persistence.

After a few days, Dhirajlal once again went to his friend's house and asked him to pay him up. But Boghāśā, was ready with his "mew". "To me also?" asked Dhirajlal. "Why not?" Said Boghāśā. "To your father even!"

Dhirajlal was very sorry he had shown him the way out of his difficulty, but repentance came too late, for, the chance was past.

Moral: How often do men incur uncalled for liabilities on the assurances of persons whose later conduct proves them to be unworthy of confidence and hence bring misery and disaster on themselves?

Cf. "If you trust before you try"; "You may repent before you die"; "The Kite and the Pigeons." — *Aesop's Fables.*

[63] *Vaidya* = A native physician.

Story 45

Can't Help It, My Friend; for, I have the Misfortune to be a Pāṭīdār

There lived in Nariāḍ a Pāṭīdār named Lālbhāī. Like their brother landholders, the Rājpūts, the Pāṭīdār keep their ladies in *pardā*, take opium and sweetmeats in company twice a day and spend a lot on the occasion of a death, marriage or pregnancy. Poor Lālbhāī had to do all this. He had a very limited income which hardly sufficed for the maintenance of his large family; but he was bound to keep up the reputation of his ancestors and whether he could afford it or not, spend as others did. As a result of this false idea of reputation, he was overwhelmed with debt. Even at the present time, almost all Pāṭīdār are of the above type and their estates are heavily encumbered. Their "reputation" is the cause of their ruin and unless and until these thoughtless and extravagant customs are put a stop to, by the government if not by themselves, they will continue to sink never to rise again.

When Lālbhāī went out in the evening he was always accompanied by half a dozen attendants and as became a Pāṭīdār, he carried a silver-*hukkā* and his silk-bordered *dhotī* swept the ground – so low was it worn. Once when he was asked by a stranger why he wore the *dhotī* so low, he replied, "Can't help it, my friend; for, I have the misfortune to be Pāṭīdār!"

Moral: Idle pleasures are only temporary and evanescent and there is no solid happiness in them. Running headlong into debt makes a man miserable and his life becomes a burden to himself and others.

Story 46

The Boy who Bit His Mother

There was once a boy who, losing his father when he was very young was under the sole care of his widowed mother, she was so extremely indulgent to the fatherless child that she never reproved him even when he quarelled with other boys and got into serious mischief. The wilful and misguided child had his way in everything and was thus led into many vices among which theft stood foremost. Whenever he brought something home, his mother never inquired how he got it, but praised him for his shrewdness; and the child was thus led to believe that he was doing nothing wrong in picking up what belonged to other people.

From an ordinary thief he rose to be a notorious pick-pocket and proved a terror to society. At last he joined a gang of robbers and with them broke into a village and plundered it. The villagers rose against them and in a conflict that ensued, the boy dealt a severe blow to a villager and laid him dead at his feet.

The gang made good their escape at the time, but later on the boy was arrested by the police and dragged before a court of justice to be tried there as a murderer and being found guilty of the offence, was sentenced to be hanged. The boy was conducted to a cell, where he sat meditating upon his past life which had been passed in the commission of crimes of every description. "Had I known," thought the boy, "that it would result in this, I would never have lived as I have done. None of my relatives – not even my mother – warned me of the consequences of my evil deeds. All this has been brought upon me by my mother who not only did not utter a word against my misdeeds, but encouraged me to follow them with greater zeal. She alone is to blame for thus leading me astray and I curse her from the bottom of my heart for wilful neglect of duty. I will, however, teach her a lesson before I perish."

When the day, on which he was to be hanged, dawned, he was conducted to the place of execution and was asked if anything could be done for him. He prayed to be allowed to see his mother and say a few words to her in private. The prayer was granted and the boy approached his mother who was standing in a corner beating her breast and crying piteously. As if he wanted to confide some secret to her before he died, he drew her face towards his and bit her nose clean off! And then exclaimed. "I owe it entirely to you, wretched woman, that I die an ignomious death! It was your duty to bring me up in the path of virtue. You neglected that duty and this is the result of your neglect. Why do you weep? It is too late to grieve, for, your tears can do me no good now!" Then addressing the people, he said, "Good people, you see me here an example of shame and punishment. But it is this mother of mine who brought me to it. If she had punished me severely for the little things that I stole when I was a boy, I should not have come to the gallows as a man."

Moral: Spare the rod and spoil the child. Wicked dispositions should be checked early. To permit a serious fault in a child to go unpunished is absolute cruelty to it; and the foolish mother, who spares her son then, is preparing bitter pain for him in the future.

Story 47

Where have You been, Raliā Gaḍhavī? On a Wild Goose Chase

These lived in Rānīsar, a village near Ahmedabad, a [64]*chāraṇa* or *gaḍhavī* named Raliā. He was a bustling-do-nothing sort of fellow and cared more about other people's business than about his own. Being naturally averse to earning his bread by hard labour he managed to live on the charity of the landed proprietors of the place, who gave him a quantity of *juwār* at harvest time. This he ground into flour, boiled it with water and lived there on. He could not afford to buy vegetables, *ghee* or sugar with it.

He was so tired of this sort of food that he made up his mind to go on a visit for a week. He had a double object in so doing. First, he would get a variety of food elsewhere and second, by his absence for a week, he could save about 7 lbs. of *juwār* which he thought of selling on his return, intending to buy sweetmeats with the proceeds! With this object in view, he wandered from one place to another and returned home at the end of a week. But as chance would have it, he was accosted by half a dozen of his caste-fellows as he entered the gates of his native village. He had to take them home with him and feed them all. They consumed all that the *gaḍhavī*'s wife had laid by during her husband's absence and thus the poor fellow's castle in the air was shattered to pieces! When asked by a friend where he had been, the *gaḍhavī* replied bitterly, "On a wild goose chase, my friend!"

---

[64] *Chāraṇa* or *gaḍhavī* = Native bards.

Moral: Man proposes, God disposes.

Story 48

Nothing Venture, Nothing Gain

A Mahommedan named Fattehkhān was the headman of a village for twenty years, during which time he had not spent a pie on board and lodging, as the villagers gave him a house to live in and invited him to dinner by turns. When he retired from service, they went to see him off for 2 miles and wept bitterly at the parting, so popular was he.

Sometime later, fifteen of the villagers left for a town which was about two day's journey from their native village. In the evening of the first day, they arrived at the village where the ex-headman resided. With the intention of putting up with him for the night, they went to his house where they received a warm welcome from the owner. But in reality, the Miā was much annoyed at heart to meet so many of his old friends, all of whom must be fed, not with bread and vegetables, but with sweetmeats. For, he had enjoyed their hospitality very often during his tenure of office. At last, he hit upon a plan to avoid this necessity and said, "You wait here, my friends. I shall soon be back with *ghee*, sugar and other articles of food for you. You don't come every day and I must show you that I am anything but ungrateful." With these words he left the house and went to a friend of his named Jhālimkhān to ask his advice as to how he could get rid of his troublesome guests without giving them offence.

After some thought, Jhālimkhān said "I can show you a way and an excellent one; but it involves some risk which you must undertake. You go back to your house. I will follow you within half an hour, accompanied by half a dozen men, all armed to the teeth and make a row in front of your house. I shall ask you either to hand over the villagers to me or fight with me on their behalf and you must prefer the latter alternative. If this sham fight induces them to leave the house, well and good; if not, I shall have to wound you which may prove serious; but it will assuredly put them to flight; there is not the least doubt about it. Seeing you engaged in their cause and risking your very life for them, they will praise you more than ever when they return to their village."

"That is an excellent plan", replied Fattehkhān dubiously. "But I don't like the latter part of it. Can't you manage it without wounding me?"

"Nothing venture, nothing have." said Jhālimkhān, "you can't have gain without risk of some sort."

Fattehkhān expressed his willingness to act according to his friend's advice. He returned home and was soon followed by Jhālimkhān as previously arranged. Reaching his friend's house, Jhālimkhān asked him in a peremptory tone to hand over his guests to him, for, he said they had murdered his father years ago! To this Fattehkhān replied, "I won't deliver my guests to you as long as there is a spark of life in me. Kill me first and then have them if you can." So saying he seized his gun and rushed out. The poor villagers thought that it was a mistake and would soon be put right. But when they saw the combatants seriously engaged and their champion wounded in the arm, they took to their heels and soon disappeared! The Mahommedans stopped fighting as soon as the guests were gone. Fattehkhān's wound was not very serious; though it took about a week to heal but it saved him an expense of about ten rupees!

Moral: The ill-disposed will easily invent an excuse for wrong-doing.

Story 49

Be a Turn Coat

Once as the Collector of Ahmedabad was riding through the district, his horse took fright at something lying on the road, threw the rider and ran away. The Collector's man followed it to a village and asked a Baniā whether he had seen the horse.

"Yes, I saw it going towards the west a short while ago."

"Come along with me," said the servant, I shall let you go as soon as we have found it." I don't see why I should go with you"; replied the Baniā. "I have pointed out the direction and I can't do anything more." Then the servant resorted to threats. "I will report you to the Collector Sāheb; now, will you come or not?"

Another Baniā who happened to pass by, seeing his caste-fellow in distress, suggested to him to turn his coat. The shrewd Baniā, taking the hint, asked the Collector's man whether his master's horse had any horns, for the one he had seen had two. The man thought that the Baniā must be a fool and so he said,

"Bullocks and not horses, have horns, you fool!" It must be a bullock, then, replied the Baniā; "and I beg your pardon for having detained you so long for nothing!"

Moral: We are justified in using prudence in the ordinary occasions of life; and it is wise to aim at and acquire a certain readiness of mind, so that in cases of difficulty we may be able to do the best we can honestly for ourselves.

Story 50

The Beggar is Never Out of His Way

There once lived in Bhavnagar a Brahmin named Madhavji Bhatt who did not understand his duty as a Brahmin according to the six Śāstras and had quite forgotten the little he had learnt in his youth. He was content to follow his ancestral profession, that of begging alms and went about the town every morning uttering "Lakṣmī bless you", "Happiness attend you", "God grant you long life", and such other phrases well known to the profession. The morning trip brought him about 4 lbs. of flour and he desired nothing more. A week before and after [65]*saṅkrānti*, he wandered from village to village in quest of alms and collected a large quantity of corn and half a dozen suits of clothes. On the [66]*baleva* day, he went from

65 *Saṅkrānti* = It is a religious holiday falling about 12 January. Food and clothes are given away to the beggars on that day.

66 *Baleva* = It falls in August. The Brahmin change their sacred threads on that day.

house to house and tied a thread round everybody's arm as a preventive against evils and earned quite a number of coppers. On New Year's Day, he wished good luck to everybody whom he met and extracted silver and copper coins in return for the blessing. In winter he went round with a subscription list meant to provide him with a warm garment; in rainy season tiles for his roof and an umbrella for himself were obtained by similar means. In short Bhattjī had devised a thousand and one ways of robbing the public and there was no want of dupes who could be easily imposed upon. Thus Bhattjī amassed a fortune and built a house of his own.

The Brahmin next took to the profession of a story-teller and in order to master the various tales from the *Rāmāyaṇa* and the *Mahābhārata* – the two Indian Epics – he picked up the alphabet and later on a little reading and writing.

Once he was repeating religious legends in a temple and on the seventh day when they were finished, the people presented him with money, clothes and corn. In order to conduct the Bhattjī to his house, they seated him on an elephant, with hundreds of people walking in front of the procession. The procession was passing through a street, when Bhattjī's eyes fell on a man distributing radishes among the beggars. Although he was seated on an elephant, he could not withstand the temptation and at once asked for a radish which was given to him with the following remark: "You are seated on an elephant and have gold rings round your arm; even pearls can be had for the asking, but you ought to have considered your present position!"

Story 51

Every Rogue is at Length Outwitted

One night several thieves entered the house of a Baniā named Rāmdās who did not think it safe to oppose them, but with the intention of playing them a trick and saving his property by that means, he said to his wife, "Do you hear? I received a letter this morning, from my agent at Bombay who says that the price of mustard seed is increasing every hour and in a day or two it will rise to forty rupees a pound! We have in the house about a maund of mustard seed and I will buy up all I can get from the town tomorrow. By the bye, I saw the mustard; we have in the house, being dried on a cot in the verandah. "Have you collected and placed it in a safe corner of the house?" "No, I haven't," replied the shrewd woman; "but I'ill do it the first thing in the morning."

The thieves who had overheard them were greatly rejoiced at their good luck and leaving everything aside, they rushed to the verandah and putting every grain of mustard in a bag, they made away with it. Then after playing the fox with the robbers, the Baniā quietly went to sleep, congratulating himself on the fertility of his brain.

The next morning, the thieves gave the bag of mustard seed to their agent and sent him to the bazaar to sell it, thinking it would bring them at least 1,000 rupees. The agent went from shop to shop showing sample; but was nowhere offered more than two rupees a maund which was all he had. He went at last to the shop of the rightful owner of the mustard and asked him at what rate he would buy it. The Baniā offered a rupee per maund, at which the agent exclaimed, "I hear that mustard is getting scarce in Bombay and the rates have therefore risen tremendously." "It was so, last night," replied the Baniā; "but they have gone down rapidly since then." He then followed the agent to the thieves' den and had them arrested and punished.

Moral: Deceit deserves to be deceived. The stratagem of the Baniā is excusable when the evil design of the thieves is considered. The disappointment of the latter does not win our sympathy; for, the Baniā had a narrow escape from their clutches.

Story 52

"There is Difference between Man and Man", says Anand to Permanand; "for, One cannot be had for Money, While Another is Not Worth a Pie"

There was a wealthy merchant in Porbunder whose shop was managed by an old and trustworthy [67]*munīm*. As the *munīm* was a thorough businessman and had an extensive experience of every department of trade, the [68]Śeṭh left him the sole management of the shop. He was handsomely remunerated for his services and was treated as one of the family.

The [69]Śeṭhānī, however, did not like the *munīm* to be so treated, while her brother was sitting without employment. She wished her brother to be appointed to the *munīm*'s place and

67 *Munīm* = The manager of a shop.

68 Śeṭh = Master.

69 Śeṭhānī = Śeṭh's wife.

never failed to make a suggestion to that effect whenever an opportunity presented itself. Once, when the Śeṭh was praising the tact and honesty of the *munīm*, his wife angrily exclaimed, "What is there in that man that you praise him so much? It is working that makes a workman. If you appoint my brother in his place, he will do the work equally well, if not better." Although the Śeṭh knew that his brother-in-law was a senseless dolt, he gave him the *munīm*'s post in order to please his wife and show her that the fellow was no good. He explained the situation to his faithful servant and asked him not to attend the shop for a week.

After the new *munīm* had been appointed in his office, the Śeṭh sent him one morning to buy 500 cans of *ghee* that had arrived for sale the previous night. He went and came back three or four times. Once to report the rates, a second time, the quality of the *ghee*, a third time, the current market rates and so on. In the mean time, the old *munīm* bought and re-sold the whole lot and earned about 500 rupees by the transaction. He sent the whole profit to the Śeṭh informing him that the *ghee* was bought and sold in his name. When the Śeṭh reported this to his better-half, she said, "Practice makes a man perfect. You try my brother for some time and he will prove equally useful."

The Śeṭh had a daughter twelve years of age. To find a suitable husband for her, the Śeṭh resolved to send his brother-in-law. He called him and said, "Go to Bhavnagar, Jūnāgaṛh and other places in Kāṭhiāwāṛ and try to find out a suitable husband for your niece. He must be of good family, well educated and sixteen years old." To make himself sure of every detail, the brother-in-law asked, "supposing I fail to find a boy sixteen years old, will two, each of eight years do?!" As the Śeṭh did not want two husbands for his daughter, he asked his obliging brother-in-law to remain at home and mind his own business.

One morning, the Śeṭh had a severe attack of fever, so his wife sent her brother to call a physician. On his way to the physician's house, the new *munīm* began to say to himself, "My sister and her husband often tell me that the ex-*munīm* used to do a number of things at a time. I will show them today that I am also capable of doing the same. The Śeṭh is very ill and the case may prove fatal! They will then require bamboo, cotton-thread and cocoanuts to prepare the [70]*nanāmī* for him! What if I buy these things in advance? It would save so much trouble later on!" He asked the physician to go at once to the house and himself went to the bazaar and bought everything that he thought would be useful in case the Śeṭh died!

As a rule such things are bought after a person is dead. Now several people had seen the *munīm* make purchases and they naturally thought that the Śeṭh must have breathed his last. So they followed him to his house bemoaning the Śeṭh's death, though he was still in the land of the living! When the mistress of the house saw people coming to attend the funeral ceremony, she summoned her brother to her presence and dismissed him with the following words, "Leave the house this moment and never show your face here again. I now fully recognize the truth of my husband's statement that there is difference between man and man."

---

70 *Nanāmī* = Lit. means "unnameable", a bamboo bier for the dead.

Story 53

A Cross and Perverse Miā

There was once a Mahommedan named Adekhān who never gave a straight and direct answer to any question that was asked him, even if it were for his own good. Two *paṇḍits* named Dhīrajram and Sūrajrām were one day discussing the tendencies of human nature, when the former said, "If we treat others with respect and kindness, we are sure to receive a similar treatment in return; for, 'kindness begets kindness' – is the law of nature. I have no faith in persons who find fault with others, for they find everything yellow, because their own eyes are jaundiced." "You may be right," replied the other, "but persons naturally inclined to vice are reclaimed with difficulty, you might as well try to keep ducks from water. For myself, I am of opinion that what is crooked by nature is never made straight by education."

As the two friends, a few days after the above discussion, were passing along a street they met Adekhān with his son, coming from the opposite direction. To prove the truth of his statement, Sūrajrām accosted the Miā, "Good morning, Miā Sāheb". "You must have some business with me"; replied the Miā suspiciously; "or you would not salute me, I am sure."

"You are mistaken, my friend; I have no business with you. We meet after a very long time and I am very glad to see you."

" I see you almost every day"; growled the Miā; "You must be blind not to see me, you book-worm!"

"Is that your son?" said Sūrajrām.

"Is he yours then? snapped the Miā. "What an idiot you are?"

"The boy looks intelligent, "replied Sūrajrām without losing his temper; "but a little delicate. Why don't you give him some tonic medicine?"

That is no business of yours! suppose he is reduced to a skeleton; what have you to do with it?"

"Excuse me, Miā Sāheb. I meant no offence. I wish him a long and happy life", responded Sūrajrām.

"As if it were in your hands to grant people long lives! kill him today if you can!"

"Well, let that pass. I have forgotton your name. What is it?"

"What is that to you?"

"My good man," said Sūrajrām, "what is the good of giving cross answers to the polite inquiries of a friend?"

"Who are you that you should call me bad names? I will be cross, perverse, obstinate, anything I choose. Take care how you utter another word."

While they were thus talking, a well-known character named Bhaglo happened to pass by. Sūrajrām stopped him and pointing him out to the Miā, said, "If you say one word, such as you have said to me, to the gentleman here he will make you open your eyes very wide."

"What do I care for him?" Replied the Miā, "am not afraid of such hedge-born brats!"

At this, Bhaglo, without more ado dealt him a severe blow on the head, levelling him to the earth and the Miā gathering himself up very slowly quietly went home.

Story 54

You are Fed with Ghee and Molasses and Yet You won't Walk Well!

In the service of one of the native states of Kāṭhiāwāṛ, there was an Arab named Abuddha. He was once sent as an escort with a bullock cart loaded with money bags to be delivered to a banker living in another town. With his gun and scimitar the Arab was following the cart, when his foot slipped on a fresh cow dung cake lying on the road. The Arab fell flat on the ground and his companions began to laugh at him. The Arab was so enraged at this that he took out his scimitar and striking the foot that had slipped, exclaimed, "Take this, then. I feed you as well as your twin brother meaning the other foot – with *ghee* and molasses and yet you won't walk well!" This thoughtless act rendered him quite unfit for further travel on foot. The driver, however, offered him a seat by his side and put him down at his house on their return. The wound took a fortnight to heal, but it did not cure the wild Arab of his thoughtless conduct.

The Arabs are as faithful and honest as they are stupid and peevish.

Story 55

There was Rāma and there was Rāvaṇa. Rāvaṇa carried away Rāma's Wife and the Latter took His Life and Kingdom. That's the Sum and Substance of the Rāmāyaṇa

A Brahmin was reading aloud to the public the legend of *Rāmāyaṇa* night after night. One night, three or four Mahommedan opium-eaters happened to pass by the place with *hukkās* in their hands. "What was this Brahmin been doing for so long a time? Asked one of the Miās of his companions.

"These Brahmin are very fond of making much out of nothing", replied the person appealed to. "They deceive the ignorant people by making a mountain of a molehill", added the third. "But do you know what he has been telling them for the last six months? They call it the *Rāmāyaṇa*, the long and short of which is that there was Rāma and there was Rāvaṇa. Rāvaṇa carried away Rāma's wife and the latter deprived him of his life and kingdom. That is the sum and substance of the *Rāmāyaṇa*. To tell this short story, the fellow has taken six months and I suppose he will take as many more!"

Story 56

Avarice is the Root of All Evils

A Baniā named Maṅgaldās was so very selfish and avaricious that money was his only God and he worshipped it day and night. He did not care for other people's feelings or interests and never hesitated to sacrifice them if his own object was served by doing so. He never listened to any other music but the chink of silver to gain which he would do anything and everything. He never did a kindness to his friends or relatives, much less to strangers. He would gladly accompany you to the bazaar if you wanted to make purchases, for he was in league with all the merchants of the place who gave him a percentage on all that was bought and sold through him. Not even his most intimate friends escaped this taxation.

One evening as Maṅgaldās was returning from a neighbouring village, he came to a river which had to be crossed in order to gain the opposite bank. The waters were very deep and there was no bridge. Maṅgaldās resolved, therefore, to swim across the river; but by the time he arrived in the middle of the stream, he was quite exhausted and the rapid and forcible current dragged him towards the mouth of the river. A few villagers, who had come to see the tide, observed the Baniā and one of them said to another, "The poor Baniā will soon perish. You are a fast swimmer and can save him if you will", "You don't know," replied the person appealed to, "he never does a thing unless he has some definite object to gain. Besides, he has never in his life helped a fellow creature, so why should others endanger their lives for him? I am sure he has fallen into the river to take out something and he must abide by the consequences."

So saying they stayed where they were and quietly observed the struggle. The helpless Baniā fought hard for his life, but at last perished in the struggle.

Moral: Do to others as you would be done by; that is the perfect standard for the guidance of men in their dealings with each other. It is a righteous retribution when the conduct we mete out to others is measured back to ourselves. Where villany goes before, vengeance follows after.

Story 57

Call Me An Ass

Once upon a time a villager was driving a bullock cart full of hay, from one village to another. On the way he fell in with a [71]Kāṭhī who begged him to give him a seat in the cart. "I will take you up on one condition," replied the villager; "I am very much afraid of that *hukkā* in your hand. The wind is blowing hard and a spark of fire from your *hukkā*-bowl will reduce all my hay to ashes in no time; but if you put out the fire, I have no objection to taking you with me."

"I'ill take great care of the bowl," said the Kāṭhī. "You need have no concern about it."

"I am not so sure of that. A tiny spark is sure to set the whole cart ablaze. I am not prepared to take that risk."

---

[71] Kāṭhī = A class of landholders from whom Kāṭhiāwāṛ (land of the Kāṭhīs) takes its name.

"But I assure you that I won't let a spark fly out and burn your hay," urged the Kāṭhī.

"But what if the worst comes to the worst?"

"Call me an ass if it turns out to be so!"

"Calling you an ass will do me no good", responded the villager. "So, to be on the safe side, I won't have you in my cart."

So saying he drove on leaving the Kāṭhī behind.

Moral: We must be careful in whom we put our trust and not imagine that those, whose general character is bad, will show exceptional favour and kindness to ourselves.

Story 58

All the Gods will Slowly Disappear, Leaving behind Them the Idols of Wood and Stone

In a certain Jain temple, where the ceremonies were performed by a man named Dāhyo, the images of the 24 [72]*tīrthaṅkar*s were all made of gold and silver with the exception of that of [73]Pārśvanāth which was made of marble and surrounded by wooden idols.

Dāhyo could not withstand the temptation of making all this gold and silver his own and made away with an image

[72] *Tīrthaṅkars* = The 24 gods of the Jains.

[73] Pārśvanāth = One of the 24 gods of Jains.

every week. He melted it and sold it secretly in distant towns to avoid detection.

After half a dozen idols had been stolen in this way, the Jains noticed that they were missing; they summoned Dāhyo before them and asked him to explain the disappearance of their gods. "I had a dream," said the sly *pujārī* (Dāhyo), "a month ago, when the *tīrthaṅkar*s plainly told me that they were heartily tired of this world and its inhabitants and would shortly leave them. They seem to have kept their word and I fear the rest will do the same in a short time! but I am forgetting to tell you one thing. At my earnest prayer to leave at least one for us to worship, they promised to leave us the marble image of Pārśvanāth and the surrounding wooden idols!" The silly *śrāvak*s (Jains) believed every word of this fabrication and trembled at the divine wrath to which they had fallen victims.

The dishonest *pujārī* at once made away with the remaining images and left the stone one to take care of itself.

Moral: Credulous persons are the prey of crafty ones.

Story 59

Jack would Wipe His Nose if He had One!

A Mahommedan named Khadū used to fetch a bundle of hay from the fields every morning and maintain himself and family on what it brought him. His body had never felt the touch of new clothes, nor had his feet ever experienced the luxury of shoes. Although the Miā was in such a miserable condition, pride lurked under his threadbare cloak. He quarrelled with his wife all day long and beat and abused her for nothing.

One day the bundle of hay did not fetch sufficient money to buy food for the whole day and the Miā had therefore to go without supper at night. As if it were the fault of his wife, he took her to task and began to abuse her right and left. "I had nothing in the house, or I would have cooked it for you," meekly said the *bībī* (wife), "it is no use abusing me for what is no fault of mine." "It is not my fault either," said the Miā indignantly; "if you won't keep quiet, I'll break your head with my shoes." "But where on earth have you got them?" appropriately remarked the *bībī*; "buy a pair first and then talk of breaking my head with them!"

The Miā was silenced by this just and appropriate retort.

Story 60

The Handle of the Axe is the Destruction of Its Progenitor

A woodcutter went one day into a forest with only the blade of an axe, to fell trees. The trees, instead of being sorry at their approaching destruction, began to laugh loudly; for, they knew very well that the blade by itself could do them no harm. The woodcutter tried the blade on every tree, but without success. He returned home much dejected and related his misfortune to his friends. They advised him to get handle of wood attached to the blade, before he next went into the woods. He at once went to a joiner, got a strong handle of wood fixed to the blade and went to the woods next morning. When the trees saw him, they began to weep and say to each other, "Now that one of us, meaning the handle which is made of wood, has gone over to the enemy, we are sure to be ruined." The woodcutter began to hack and hew without distinction and a heap of the noblest trees lay at his feet in no time.

Moral: A house divided against itself cannot stand. The tale is intended to show the evils of family disunion. Quarrels are at all times odious; how much more so when they take place among those bound by the ties of blood, duty, nature, relationship and self-interest to be the allies and protectors of each other?

Story 61

A Niche in the Wall

A Mahommedan named Tīsmārkhān was brought to such a state of poverty that he prepared to dispose of the house in which he lived. There was a niche in the wall of one of the rooms which the Miā kept to himself, while the rest of the building was sold to a Baniā. It was plainly stated in the document of sale that the niche dedicated to a [74]*pīr* and situated in such and such a room was the Miā's and that he could make what use he would of it. Failing to perceive the

[74] *Pīr* = A saint.

Miā's motive in reserving such a right in the house to himself, the Baniā did not object to it.

A week after the Baniā came into possession of the house, the Miā went there and after burning incense and offering prayers to the *pīr*, went away. On the following Friday, he went to the house with half a dozen Muslims who had vows to perform, so he said, to the *pīr*. The Baniā objected to give admission to so many persons, but the Miā referred him to the deed and claimed entrance as a matter of right. The Baniā had no alternative but to quietly put up with the inconvenience and trouble which he himself had brought upon his family.

Things were going on in this way, when the time came for the performance of the marriage ceremony of the Baniā's only son. In the evening of the marriage guests began to pour in and were arranged in two rows. Sweetmeats and vegetables were served and the host was exhorting them to do full justice to the fare when the Miā accompanied by a number of Musalmāns broke in like a bolt from the blue. He peremptorily asked the Baniā to let him pass on to the niche of his *pīr* where he had to sacrifice a goat that night. The poor Baniā was in a fix. He could not allow the Miā to pass as that would pollute the whole caste, nor could he refuse him the admission to which he was entitled. Again the killing of a goat in the house, where the sacred marriage ceremony was to be performed, was a sin that would tell heavily against the newly-united couple. The guests came to the Baniā's help and asked the Miā on what terms he would resign his right to the niche. The Miā, who had all along been waiting for this opportunity, demanded as much for the small hole in the wall as he had received for the whole house. The Baniā had to satisfy the demand, unjust and unreasonable as it was, to escape further molestation. From that day the Baniā resolved to think twice before he acted.

Moral: Experience teaches. No second warning is required to teach a wise man to eschew what he has once proved to be hurtful. A burnt child naturally dreads the fire.

Story 62

Sticking Fast to a Thing

There lived in Peṭlād a Kunbī named Hari Patel. He was one of the leading persons of his caste and was often appointed an arbitrator in caste disputes; he had an only son named Bhago who was a great blockhead and knew very little about the world and its ways. When the Patel was on his deathbed he summoned Bhago before him and addressed him as follows: "My son, I have not long to live in this world; what I grieve moat about is what will become of you after I have passed away. You are too stupid to look after yourself and there is nobody to whose care I can safely entrust you. If you, however, assure me that you will mend your ways I shall die contented." Bhago, who was not a bad boy at heart, was overcome by the appeal of his dying parent and solemnly promised to follow his advice to the very letter; whereupon the father said, "sticking fast to a thing is the surest way to success. Patience and perseverance will overcome a mountain. Remember this, there are difficulties in the way of attaining most things worth having; but they are only placed there to be overcome, to be subdued not to be shunned from fear or turned from in idleness."

Bhago promised his father that from that day he would stick fast to everything he undertook and he religiously kept his promise. Soon after this the Patel died leaving Bhago to guide himself as best as he could.

One day in the rainy season as Bhago was sowing *bājarī* in his field, he saw an ass enter his field from the opposite side. Bhago ran after it club in hand and seized the mischievous fellow by the tail. The ass brayed and kicked but Bhago "stuck fast" to it. In order to get free, the ass kicked Bhago right and left and hurt him in several places, but he would not let go his hold. He suffered himself to be dragged through the streets of Peṭlād and laughed at by the people, but he did not for a moment think of violating the sacred promise made to his father on his deathbed! Being much bruised, he at last became unconscious and it was only then that the tail slipped out of his hands.

Moral: It is wise to consider a course of conduct in all its bearings before we determine on it. We must weigh well the consequences before we jump at a thing.

Story 63

So Got, So Gone

A milkmaid living in a village used to go every morning and evening to a neighbouring town to sell milk. For a few months she supplied her customers with pure and fresh milk and established her reputation as an honest dealer, until at last her custom rose so high that the milk she brought fell short of demand. In order to meet the growing demand, she, one day, mixed, with the milk, some water from a rivulet that lay between her village and the town. The mixture was soon disposed of and with money in her pot, she left the town for her native place. On her way, she stopped on the bank of the rivulet to drink some water. After satisfying her thirst, she took the money out of the pot and after counting it, deposited it on the bank and began to wash the milk-pot.

Now it so happened that a kite, thinking it to be some sort of food, pounced upon the coppers and seizing as many as her beak could hold flew away. The milkmaid began to cry and beat her breast at this sudden loss and was cursing her fate when the kite let fall the money into the rivulet, on which another milkmaid, who had noticed the adulteration that morning, remarked, "Why do you weep, sister? You must know that cheating never prospers and craft brings nothing home. In fact, you have lost nothing; for, to naught it has gone that came from naught." This silenced the woman and from that day she left off mixing water with milk.

Moral: How often do men give up honour and future prosperity for a temporary pleasure or gain! They don't see that the retribution of their sin cannot fail to overtake them in the end. They must know that honesty is the best policy.

Story 64

A Boon Asked by a Blind Man

There lived in Somnāth Pāṭan a Baniā named Rāmdās. Small-pox had deprived him of his eyesight when he was a mere child and to add to his misfortunes, his parents died leaving him quite helpless and dependent on public charity. At last a pious man took compassion on him and provided him with a free board and lodging at his house. He also taught him to sing religious, hymns and in a short time, he learnt a number of them by heart, as the blind naturally have a very retentive memory.

One day as the blind Baniā was singing hymns in the temple of Somnāth, [75]Śaṅkara was so very pleased with his devotion that he appeared before him and commanded him to ask a boon. The Baniā was overjoyed at his good luck and began to revolve in his mind what he had best demand. "If I seek back my eyesight", thought he, "it would still leave me a poor man. If I demand riches, how can I enjoy them without eyesight? Again I am a bachelor. If I ask for a wife, what are we to live upon? Śaṅkara never grants two favours at a time. I must therefore frame my demand in such terms as will include all that I want and still look like one demand." When, therefore, asked again by Śaṅkara to demand a boon, he said, "Mighty Lord of the Universe, if you are really pleased with me I have no other desire" but "to see my youngest son's wife churning cream in a gold pot on the seventh storey of my house!" This meant eyesight, a wife, sons more than one, riches, a palatial building and much else. Śaṅkara had to grant all these things

[75] Śaṅkara = The third of the Hindu Triad. The Destroyer.

to keep his promise, but from that day he thought twice before he made a promise to a Baniā!

Story 65

The Bhāṭs of Mehsānā, Dine to Morrow

There is a large population of Bhāṭs in Mehsānā who in ancient time claimed, as a matter of right, to be fed when there was a caste-dinner among the Baniās. As it was thought very unreasonable and expensive, the Baniās had wisely stopped the caste-dinners altogether. Once, however, a rich Baniā resolved to give a caste-dinner and exclude the Bhāṭs therefrom. With this object, he issued invitations among the Baniās only.

When the Bhāṭs heard this, they proceeded in a body to the [76]Śeṭh's house and sat there fasting in order to enforce their claim. The [77]*mahājana*, however, did not listen to them; whereupon the Bhāṭs took to extreme measures and with swords and knives in hand, they threatened the Baniās that if they persisted in not feeding them, they would shed their own blood and the sin would devolve upon the Baniā's heads. This was too much for the Baniās and in order to stop bloodshed they promised the Bhāṭs to feed them the next day. The Bhāṭs were not, however, to be taken in like that, but replied that

[76] Śeṭh = A leader among the Baniās.

[77] *Mahājana* = Leading person of the Baniā community.

they must have the promise in black and white. A document was therefore prepared in which were written the following words: "The Bhāṭs of Mehsānā dine tomorrow". Neither place nor dates were mentioned. The *mahājana* affixed their signs manual to it and the Bhāṭs returned to their places to prepare for the next day's feast.

The next morning the Bhāṭs went to the *mahājana* and demanded a large quantity of flour, *ghee* and sugar to prepare sweet balls. The *mahājana* laughed at them and asked them with surprise in their looks what right they had to make such a foolish demand. "We have your promise in black and white," angrily exclaimed the Bhāṭs, "and we won't let you escape it." "And what does that promise say?" Asked one of the Baniās. "That the Bhāṭs of Mehsānā dine tomorrow"; "Well, then why do you come today?" Asked the Baniās. "Because the promise was made yesterday," retorted the Bhāṭs. "Does the document bear yesterday's date? Demanded the Baniās, the Bhāṭs referred to the document but there was no date in it. So they said, "Never mind the document. We have your word and that is enough." "That comes too late, my friends," said the Baniās; "we are prepared to carry out whatever is written on that paper. You had better leave us at present and come when the promise falls due."

This curt reply struck the Bhāṭs dumb. They tore the paper to pieces and went away.

Moral: Force without foresight is of no avail. The chief excellency of man consists in fertility of invention and discovery of resources and expedients in situations of danger and difficulty.

Story 66

Who is the Wiser of the Two?

There was in a native state of Gujarat a Kunbī named Gāndo Patel who owned several acres of land and was, moreover, the headman of his caste.

Once on New Year's Day, Gāndo Patel sent his son to the Kutcheri with sugar and cocoanut to be offered to the king as is the custom among the native states of India. The young Patel, after performing the [78]*Rām-Rām* ceremony, placed the cocoanut and the sugar at the king's feet whereupon the latter ordered his attendants to give the Patel [79]*pān-sūpārī* and *uttar*. The country bred Kunbī had never in his life seen *uttar*, so he received it in the hollow of his hand and thinking it to be sacred water of some sort, he first applied it to his eyes and forehead and then licked it off! This made the whole Kutcheri roar with laughter.

A few days later, Gāndo Patel went to the king on some business connected with his land, when the king referred to the *uttar* incident and advised the Patel to teach manners to his son. "He is a stupid boy, my linege," said the Patel, "or he would not have used the costly *uttar* in that way! if I were in his place, I would have taken it home and eaten it with *bājarī*-bread!" The king could not help laughing at the Patel's ignorance and was at a loss to decide whether the father or the son was the wiser!

---

78 *Rām-Rām* = God bless you.

79 *Pān-sūpārī* and *uttar* = Betel leaf and otto or essence of flowers.

Story 67

Waging War Against the Sun!

A certain village of Gujarat, chiefly inhabited by Mahommedan landowners, was under British jurisdiction and the government offices were situated in a town 5 miles from the village; so that the Miās had to go there very often. As a rule, they took their breakfast, consisting of a large dose of opium and a larger one of sweetmeats, after sunrise and then leisurely proceeded to the town with *hukkās* in their hands. After doing business in the town, they left it in the afternoon, after another dose of opium and sweetmeats.

As the town was situated due east from the village, they had to put up with the burning rays of the sun which played directly on their faces at both times of the day.

Once in summer, as the Miās were returning from the town in the afternoon, they felt the heat so trying that the first thing they resolved to do on reaching home was to hold a meeting to discuss the means of effectually stopping the mischievous pranks of the sun. The meeting was accordingly held and it was unanimously resolved to declare war against the sun.

Next morning all the Mahommedans of the place armed themselves with swords and spears and bows and arrows and marched out of the village gate to meet the common foe in the open field! A Baniā, who had seen the martial procession move out, followed them to the village gate and approaching the general of the warlike band, he said, "It is not fair to march against an enemy without previously informing him of your intention. Again, seeing you in earnest, he will most probably come to terms and spare you unnecessary trouble." "But who will take our message to him and settle the dispute amicably?" asked the general. "I will do that for you, if you promise to pay me 500 rupees after I have amicably settled the dispute." The Miās agreed to the proposal, went home and eagerly awaited the Baniā's return.

At night fall the Baniā came back with a radiant face and exclaimed, "I have succeeded. He wouldn't listen to me at first, but when I mentioned your name he actually trembled with fear. He has, however agreed to keep away from your path on one condition and I am sure you won't object to it. He wishes you to reverse the order of your journey, that is to go to the town in the afternoon and return there from in the morning!"

The Miās accepted the condition and tried the experiment on the following day. The sun no longer faced them and they were quite satisfied. The Baniā received the stipulated sum and went home inwardly chuckling at his ingenuity and laughing at the Miās for their stupidity.

Moral: The tale teaches a double lesson. That every fool is at last found an ass; and that we must beware of self-interested advisers.

Story 68

Who can Spin so Much Cotton?

Bībījān, a Mahommedan widow of Ahmedabad, earned bread for herself and daughter by spinning cotton on a country wheel at which she worked from morning till night, turning out about 1/2 lb. of fine thread which she sold to the weavers. The spinning wheels and weaving looms were all worked with hand as nobody know anything about spinning and weaving mills worked by steam power. This manual labour afforded daily bread to so many widows and orphans that the one-meal-a-day state of things and starvation were unknown in those days. Much of the Indian cotton was then exported to England, for; the product was much in excess to the consumption.

Once Bībījān went to Cambay to see her parents. As she was one day walking on the [80]*bunder* with her daughter, the girl's eyes fell on a large ship laden with bales and she asked her mother what they contained and where they were taking them. "They contain cotton, my dear," replied the mother, "and they send them to [81]Vilāyat to be spun and woven into cloth." "My lord!" exclaimed the girl, "who can spin so much cotton?

Vilāyat must surely be a country inhabited by widows only!"

Moral: They that be in hell think there's no heaven.

Story 69

It is Your Mace that Commands Respect, not You

There was, in the service of a native prince, a mace-bearer who oppressed the people very much; his chief business being to get unpaid labourers for the state. This was like

80 *Bunder* = A sea-port; here it means seashore.

81 Vilāyat = Lit. means "Home", England being the home of the Englishmen is known as Vilāyat in this country.

putting a naked sword in a mad man's hand. He was a terror to the poor who ran away at the mere sight of him. They dared not complain against him to the king, for he was a royal favourite and they had, therefore, no other alternative but to patiently submit to his rod of iron.

One evening the mace-bearer went to [82]Ḍheḍhwāḍā to get hold of some Ḍheḍhas for [83]*veṭha*. The poor Ḍheḍhas had just returned from a hard day's work and were quite tired out. When, therefore, asked by the mace-bearer to go with him, they humbly replied that as they were quite exhausted, they would do his bidding in the morning. But the mace-bearer was not a man to be thrilled with. He began to abuse and beat them right and left. Being unable to stand this sort of thing any longer, one of the Ḍheḍhas came forward and spoke as follows: "Do your worst, man. We won't move an inch hence. We would show you what stuff we are made of, but that mace in your hand disarms us. Put that aside and see what we can do." The mace-bearer threw down the mace and commanded the Ḍheḍhas in his own name to go with him that instant. Seeing him reduced to the same level as themselves, the Ḍheḍhas attacked him in a body and beat him to their hearts' content.

The mace-bearer lodged a complaint against the Ḍheḍhas who were summoned to the court. In defence they related the previous day's occurrence and added that the mace-bearer was guilty of insulting the king for having thrown down the royal mace. The king at once dismissed the high-handed and oppressive officer and rewarded the Ḍheḍhas for their moral courage.

---

[82] Ḍheḍhwāḍā = A place inhabited by Ḍheḍhas.

[83] *Veṭha* = Forced labour.

Moral: Where rulers are mere figure-heads and the officers deal falsely and exercise cruelty the state does not prosper.

Story 70

He That Shows His Purse Longs to be Rid of It

There lived in Navsārī a [84]*mochī* named Fulio who was a great miser. At the end of thirty years of hard labour and strict economy he had amassed 999 rupees – a fortune to a man of his position. These rupees he neither put out to interest nor kept them in a box in his house. He dug a deep hole in the cowshed just under a nail and putting the rupees in an earthen jar and sealing its mouth with wheat paste; he buried it 4 ft deep.

Fulio was considered a very rich man in his caste. The first and the only question, he put to every customer that came to his shop, was how much ready cash he owned. If it was more than 999, he would keep quiet; but if it chanced to be less, he would laugh at its possessor and call him a comparatively poor man. The words "nine hundred and ninety-nine" were on the top of his tougue and were repeated twice in an hour. Everybody in the town knew what Fulio was worth, but nobody was aware of the whereabouts of the nine hundred and ninety-nine.

One day, two persons of very questionable reputation went to Fulio's shop and after giving the measurement of their feet for a couple of pairs of shoes, they purposely inferred to the

[84] *Mochī* = A shoe-maker.

capital and capitalists of the town. Fulio at once asked them what they themselves were worth. The nocturial knights said very hesitatingly that they were very poor and did not own more than 500 rupees between them. "That's nothing," said Fulio; "I have with me at this moment 999 rupees." The thieves made as if they doubted the truth of Fulio's statement and said, "There is neither a box nor a cupboard in your house. Where on earth do you keep such a large sum?" "In the cowshed, under the nail," replied Fulio promptly; "that's the safest place; for, nobody would look for rupees there."

After talking for a while, the customers took their leave. At midnight they broke into Fulio's compound and digging out the rupees, they made away with them. The next morning, Fulio found to his grief that the rupees were stolen. He had nobody but himself to blame, for, his misfortune was of his own creation.

Moral: A fool and his money are soon parted. Many of the troubles of life are brought on men by their own faults.

Story 71

A Learned Fool

There lived in Sojitrā, a village in Gujarat, a learned Brahmin named Gafalshanker. He was well-versed in the Vedas and maintained sacrificial fire in his house. He had an only son named Vidyādhara whom he wished to bring up as a [85]*vediā*. When Vidyādhara was seven years of age, the sacred-thread ceremony was performed and in the following year he was married to a girl of a good family.

Immediately after marriage the boy was sent to Kāśī to study the Vedas and other religious books. There he lived with a [86]*guru* who gave him free board and lodging and imparted tuition free of charge. In return for this tremendous obligation, Vidyādhara had to go a-begging for the *guru* every morning and do all sorts of work for the [87]*gorānī*; cleaning the cooking pots, sweeping the house and washing the clothes were among the work he did for the household.

At the end of ten years of hard labour mental and physical, he was examined by it committee of learned Brahmin who asked him to repeat a number of *śloka*s which he did like a parrot. He was declared successful and the degree of *paṇḍit* was conferred upon him. He, then, took leave of his *guru* and *gorānī* and left for his native village.

One fine morning, after two months' journey on foot, he approached Sojitrā, his native village and sat down beneath a banyan tree, that grew on the bank of the river, to take rest. A Baniā boy, who was of the same age as Vidyādhara and who knew him well, happened to pass by at the time. As soon as he caught sight of his old companion, he ran to him and the friends were soon locked in each other's embrace. After a while the Baniā asked the Brahmin how far he had studied to which the latter replied that he knew all the Vedas by heart. The following conversation then took place between them.

---

85 *Vediā* = One well-versed in the Vedas.

86 *Guru* = A religious preceptor.

87 *Gorānī* = *Guru*'s wife.

"Are my people all right?" asked the *paṇḍit*. "Yes they are, with one exception."

"And what is that?"

"You just take off your clothes and stand in the bed of the river; then I'll tell you what it is", responded the Baniā.

The *paṇḍit* did as he was asked to do and then asked Baniā what it was. The Baniā said with a grave face, "your wife has become a widow!"

"Poor woman, I am much grieved to hear that." So saying the Brahmin began to weep piteously. The Baniā consoled him and advised him to cover his face with a cloth and go home weeping. The learned fool did so and sat at the door of his house weeping loudly. The noise attracted the inmates of the house. With great trouble they stopped him crying and taking him indoors, asked him the cause of his so doing. "You know the reasons as well as I do," said the *paṇḍit*; "Why did you not inform me at Kāśī that my poor wife was widowed?" His widowed sister who was standing by could not help laughing at the simplicity of her brother. "How is that possible, you idiot?" She remarked. "She can't be a widow as long as you are in the land of the living!"

"What has my life or death to do with her widowhood?" Argued the *paṇḍit*; "why, take your own case. They call you a widow in spite of my being alive! What prevents my wife then from being so called?!"

Moral: A handful of common sense is better than a bushel of learning. There is a saying and a true one that "knowledge without practice makes but half an artist". Read not books alone but men.

Story 72

Half the [88]Juwār belongs to Miā

A Mahommedan named Rasūlkhān was the [89]Kotwāl of Pālanpur, a town, which formed a part of the Mogul Empire. Rasūlkhān lived there as the only representative of the Mogul Emperor and was entrusted with judicial as well as executive powers. Unlike his caste fellows, he was a politician of no mean abilities, an instance of which is given below.

A Baniā was once getting a cellar cleaned and plastered for the storage of *juwār*, as a provision against famine. When the cellar was filled to the brim and the Baniā was preparing the account thereof to be deposited along with the *juwār* for future reference, the Kotwāl happened to pass by his house and the Baniā invited him to have a look at the cellar. After complimenting, the Baniā on his prudence and foresight, the Kotwāl picked up a grain of *juwār* from the cellar and dividing it into two pieces; he put one into the cellar and threw away the other. He then asked the Baniā to mention in the paper that half the *juwār* belonged to Miā! Suspecting this demand to be the outcome of some evil design, the Baniā at first refused to do so, but by force and persuasion, more especially the former, the Miā at last prevailed upon the Baniā to accept his share and make mention of it in the paper to be deposited along with the *juwār*.

After a decade, a disastrous famine overtook that part of Gujarat in which the Baniā resided and the prices of food grain rose fourfold. With the object of disposing of the *juwār* and

88 *Juwār* = A sort of food grain.

89 Kotwāl = A police Magistrate.

making a large profit by the sale, the Baniā opened the cellar. No sooner did the Miā hear that the cellar was opened, than he came to the Baniā's house and claimed half the quantity of *juwār* for himself. The Baniā reminded him in vain that it was not half the quantity but only half a grain of *juwār* that he had deposited in the cellar. "You may say what you like," said the wily Miā, "but fortunately for me that paper remains as an evidence in my favour!" So saying he summoned a few respectable people of the town and placed the paper before them. It was plainly stated therein that half the *juwār* belonged to Miā and the committee, who knew nothing about the matter, gave their decision in Miā's favour on the strength of that evidence in black and white. In short the Baniā had to give half the contents of the cellar to Miā for nothing.

Moral: Words may pass away and be forgotten, but that which is committed to writing will remain as evidence. We must, therefore, be very careful of what we give in black and white.

Story 73

A Shepherd always Dreams of Open Fields

There was once a shepherd named Noghan who owned some cattle and led the life of a nomad. A European gentleman once bought his cow and took the shepherd with him to Bombay to look after it. Noghan who had passed his life between villages and fields was wonderstruck with the palatial buildings of Bombay and a variety of things he had never seen in his life.

The Sāheb lived in a grand bungalow on the Appollo Bunder. The shepherd was assigned a room furnished with thick carpets, bent-wood chairs, sofas, a spring cot and a clock. The shepherd did not feel at home in the bungalow and looked much confused. After passing a few weary hours in this unknown place, he asked one of the servants where he could go to answer the call of nature. The servant led him to a latrine; but no sooner did Noghan enter it than he came back and runniug to the Sāheb he exclaimed, "That fellow there played me an evil trick. I asked him to lead me to a latrine and he took me to the kitchen instead, for, I saw a stone hearth there with my own eyes!" The Sāheb laughed at him and explained to him that it was not a kitchen but a latrine.

In the evening the Sāheb's servants took him out for a walk. But he had not moved more than a few steps from the bungalow when he stopped short in the middle of the road and asked the servants to take him back to the bungalow. When asked the reason, he pointed to several houses standing in front of him and exclaimed. "They have heaped the rooms one over another without fastening them with ropes! They are sure to come down one of these days and I won't risk my life by walking under them!"

At night Noghan did not sleep on the cot for fear of falling down. He laid himself down on the floor, but he could not sleep, the tuck tuck of the clock kept him awake for the whole night. He could not identify the sound with that of any bird or beast, tame or wild, that he had come across in the woods. He got up early next morning, went to the Sāheb's room and prayed him with tears in his eyes to let him go to his native village.

Moral: He who stays in the valley will never go over the hill.

Cf. "Give me again my hollow tree"; "A crust of bread and liberty".

Story 74

A Negro Thinks His Own Child the Handsomest

A king once asked his Negro slave to procure him the handsomest child from the town, as he had taken a vow to get one and pass it through the streets of the town in right royal pomp. The slave wandered from house to house but not a single child came up to his ideal of beauty. Quite overcome with fatigue, he at last went to his house and informed his wife of the king's order. "You ought to have come home directly," said his wife, "and taken our dear little Habib to the king; for he is the handsomest child in the whole town!" The Negro at once took the hint and went with his glossy black cherub to the royal presence. "Have you brought me the child?" asked the king impatiently. "Yes, Your Highness," replied the slave, "and here it is." "What! You call this child a handsome one!" "And why not, [90]*nāmdār*? you left the selection to me; and I have made it after wandering over the whole town." The king laughed at him and dismissed him.

---

[90] *Nāmdār* = Of great name.

Moral: Every cock is proud of his own dung-hill and every ass thinks himself worthy to stand with the king's horses.

Story 75

Come and Stay in Māliā if You are Afraid of [91]Allah

Māliā is a small town situated in the north-west of Kāṭhiāwāṛ. It is chiefly inhabited by the Miānās — a warlike though ignorant race — all Mahommedans by religion and knowing as much of the Koran as they do of the Vedas. They are creatures of impulse and killing a human being is to them like killing an ant. However, if you have once broken bread with them, they will not hurt a hair of your head as long as they live. There is honour even among robbers, they say. About ten years ago, Miānā outlaws were a terror to the whole of Kāṭhiāwāṛ, but the British officers hunted them from place to place like wild beasts and at last succeeded in capturing and packing most of them off to Port Blair, a penal settlement in the Andamans in the Bay of Bengal.

Once upon a time a Miānā was returning from a village, when his eyes fell upon an Arab performing his [92]*namāẓ*. The Miānā had never performed the *namāẓ* himself, although he was a Mahommedan, nor had he ever seen anybody performing it. He was therefore surprised to see the Arab standing up for a while, then sitting down on his knees and then prostrating

---

[91] *Allah* = God.

[92] *Namāẓ* = Prayers.

himself on the ground, muttering something all the time. He thought to himself that the Arab must be greatly troubled in mind and did not therefore know what he was about. "Whom are you afraid of, my friend?" Asked the Miānā. "Of nobody," answered the Arab. "But your movements show that you are." Urged the Miānā. "I was only offering my prayers to Allāh", replied the Arab. And who may He be and why should you pray to Him?" Asked the Miānā. "He is the giver of bread and protector of the whole Universe. He forgives our sins if we be really sorry for them and promise Him not to repeat them. He punishes the evil-doers if they don't mend their ways." I see, exclaimed the Miānā, "you pray to Him to escape punishment. Well, if you are afraid of Allah, come and stay in Māliā, for, nobody cares for Him there!"

The Arab thanked him for his kind suggestion and said he would gladly have recourse to it when he was past redemption.

Story 76

Presence of Mind is the Best Weapon

Once the emperor Akbar asked Lahūwā what was the best weapon, to which the jester replied that it depended much on the purpose for which it was required. A gun would be the best weapon to fight with from a distance, while a sword would be more useful than a gun in a hand to hand fight. "Personally I think presence of mind is the best weapon", added the jester. The Emperor was anything but satisfied with the strange reply and said that he would someday put his statement to the test.

A few days after this, the emperor was sitting in the balcony of his palace, when he saw Lahūwā coming towards the palace. He told a keeper to set an elephant free at once and goad him into the narrow lane Lahūwā had to pass through. The order was immediately obeyed. When the jester saw the elephant approaching, he at once understood that it was at the instance of the emperor that this dangerous trick was played upon him, which if not met with courage, would prove fatal. With that presence of mind for which he is so renowned in Indian History, he seized a puppy that was lying on the road and threw it at the elephant. The attention of the elephant was thus diverted for a short time, during which he made good his escape and approaching his royal master, he exclaimed, "I hope your Majesty is now convinced that presence of mind is the best weapon; for, a gun or a sword would have availed me nought at such a critical time".

Moral: A man of courage never wants weapons.

Story 77

I Would Die, if It were Only to Make You a Widow

There was a Mārwāṛī who had come to and settled in Bombay; where he started business as a petty grocer and gradually rose to be a thriving moneylender. He accomodated many a prodigal son of miserly fathers with large sums of money on "Double the principal on father's death" terms. He had come to Bombay with a score of rupees plus a few cooking pots and was now worth two hundred thousand in hard cash and as many invested in a row of houses, which brought him a good round sum every month.

Now, if you have a look at the census returns, you will find that among the Mārwāṛīs males outnumber the females. It is but natural that where the demand is greater than the supply, the commodity fetches a phenomenal price. This is exactly the case with the Mārwāṛī girl of marriageable age. She is worth her weight in gold; for, a girl in her teens, weighing about 7 stone, fetches as many as 20,000 rupees. You may call this slavery, this buying and selling of girls; but we don't care what other people call it. It is enough that we call it [93]*kanyā-dān* and it is our look out what terms to make while bestowing the gift. But I am digressing.

After a stay of over twenty years in Bombay and when he was in his fortieth year, the Mārwāṛī thought it was time to buy a wife and with the object of securing one, he went to his native place and was soon married. There is a saying that "when a woman comes in happiness flies". "The land of marriage," says a Frenchman, "has this peculiarity that strangers are desirous of inhabiting it, while its natural inhabitants would willingly be banished thence." To the poor Mārwāṛī wedlock turned out to be a real padlock. The woman proved to be a termagant and was so quarrelsome that the poor fellow knew no rest and cursed the day he was married. He had bought her for 25,000 rupees and he found out when it was too late that his wickedly acquired money was foolishly spent. He abused her and he beat her, but she took

[93] *Kanyā-dān* – Gift of bride.

care to repay it in kind and that with interest. The Mārwāṛī got at last so tired that he resolved to commit suicide and thus put an end to his unpleasant life. He communicated his intention to his better-half, thinking it would have a salutary effect, but the woman said quietly, "That does not concern me at all; you are your own master and do what you will with yourself." The Mārwāṛī was so enraged at this that he took out a knife and while dealing a blow on his throat he exclaimed, "I will die, if it were only to make you a widow". These words were scarcely out of his mouth when he fell unconscious on the ground and soon perished. His brothers took possession of his property, moveable and immoveable and the woman was given a hut to live in and repent of her sins at leisure.

Story 78

Where shall We Graze the Cattle?

Two shepherds named Śivdās and Nājo were great friends. They always went together to graze their cattle. They ate together, played together and sang [94]*dūhās* together. Śivdās's hut was on one bank of a stream while Nājo's was on the other.

Once in the month of Āṣāḍha (July), it rained very heavily all night. When Nājo rose next morning, he found the stream imfordable and he did not know where to take his cattle that day. He wanted to consult Śivdās on the point. He came out

[94] *Dūhās* = Rural songs.

of his hut and in a shrill voice peculiar to shepherds he asked Śivdās to cross over to him as he had something of importance to ask him. Fearing that the previous night's rain had done some harm to his friend's hut and cattle, the honest shepherd at once threw himself into the swollen stream and began to swim across it with great vigour. With great difficulty he managed to reach the opposite bank and dripping with water and shivering with cold, he asked his friend what he had called him for. "I would have come over to you with my cattle," said Nājo, "but the stream won't allow me to do that. I say, where shall we graze our cattle today?" Śivdās knew not whether to laugh or be angry at his friend's conduct. Assuming therefore, a serious expression he said, "You could have asked me that from where I was. There was no need of making me cross the river at the risk of my life." "I did not know that you had grown so lazy as that, or I wouldn't have called you at all!" retorted Nājo.

Moral: He who listens to a fool is a greater fool.

Story 79

To Go for Wool and Come Home Shorn

There lived in Māngrol a barber named Mālo. By hard work and strict economy, he had laid by a sum of 200 rupees. Human nature is the same all over the world and poor Mālo was no exception to it. He longed to turn his 200 into as many thousand.

This Mālo was the family barbers of many a big [95]Śeṭhiā. Barbers are known as newsmongers in every country and Mālo was a worthy member of his class. Whenever he was summoned by a Śeṭhiā on professional duty, he kept prattling from the beginning to the end of shaving operation. What each Śeṭhiā was worth and how he came by his fortune were Mālo's questions to everybody. When he was once told by one of his rich clients that he owed his fortune to trade. Mālo at once resolved to turn a trader without knowing the *A*, *B*, *C*, of the business. He asked the Śeṭhiā what he had better do. "You had better be content with what you have," said the Śeṭhiā, "for, trade is not in your line and you will never succeed in it."

The foolish barber thought that the Śeṭhiā did not wish that he should be a rich man and therefore dissuaded him from trying his hand at commerce. He, therefore, sought the advice of another Śeṭhiā who happened to be a great rogue. He knew Mālo's propensities and thought of teaching him a lesson that would bring him to his senses. One day, therefore, when Mālo as usual put him the question, he said, "I hear from my agent at Jūnāgaṛh that a company of Sepoys will shortly leave there for Māngrol. They will arrive here by the end of the week. These Sepoys are very fond of potherbs and anybody who lays in a stock of those vegetables against their arrival is sure to make a fortune. It is below my dignity and my caste-fellows would not allow me to do it, or I myself would go and buy up all potherbs to be had ten miles round and sell them to the troopers at a rupee a pound!"

Mālo hastily finished the operation, went home and with the 200 rupees in his pocket, he ran to the bazaar and bought off all the potherbs. Then he went to the surrounding villages and imported

95 Śeṭhiā = A rich merchant.

cartloads of the vegetables from thence and deposited all in a warehouse to be opened when the troops arrived. Day after day passed without any sign of the Sepoys' coming and the vegetables began to putrify. Growing impatient at last he went to the Baniā and asked him when the Sepoys were coming. "My agent," said the Baniā calmly, "is silent on the point; so, I fear they have taken another route. You know as well as I do that 'Forces and fish rush against the current'. Now that they have not reached here by this time, I don't think they will come at all!" The barber stood aghast at this unexpected news and knew not what to do with a house full of potherbs. Quite overcome by this sudden misfortune, he dragged himself home with great difficulty and with despair depicted on his face. On opening the warehouse he found the vegetables all rotten and unfit for use. He disposed them of for a few coppers to a cultivator who carted it to his field to use it as manure. The new merchant adventurer quietly returned to his old trade and never repeated the experiment.

Moral: We should never be tempted to risk the chances of a blind fortune. In the present day, every tempting wave of speculation leads people to risk its perils and they are happy if they gain prudence by the loss of their first veuture.

Story 80

She is no Gift; for, I have Paid for Her

Bhagwandas was a university man. He was a member of the Kāyastha community and his parents lived in Broach. He attended every meeting of the social conference and was a [96]*sudhārawāllāh* at heart. He strongly held that social reforms must precede political ones and his mind was therefore bent upon eradicating social evils at any cost. He began at the beginning and strove to impress upon the ignorant mass that early marriages and the sale of girls were the two potent causes of the increasing number of widows every year. He firmly held that the question of widow remarriage would to a great extent disappear if these two evils were checked in time. When the people of the old school heard him, they shook their heads and said, "He is yet a child and has not seen the world. Experience comes with age. The silly boy thinks that his ancestors were fools."

Once he was invited to a marriage party held in honour of a bridegroom aged sixty and a baby-bride of thirteen! He was so struck at the difference between their age that he gave a free expression to his feelings and left in disgust. His caste-fellows resented his conduct and came to a private understanding that none should ever propose to give his daughter in marriage to Bhagwandas. The young reformer did not in the least mind this step of theirs, but his aged father felt it very much. He longed to see his son married and settled in life before his eyes were closed. He therefore privately arranged with a needy father to give his daughter in marriage to Bhagwandas in return for 5,000 rupees paid to him in advance. Although the sale of daughters is going on, on an extensive scale at the present day and has proved a capital invention, it has not as yet gained a universal sanction and has not therefore grown into a custom. But it is making rapid strides and has made its way into most families whence it is not likely to be turned out. However that may be,

---

96 *Sudhārawāllāh* = A social reformer.

the sale of girls is looked upon as a disgrace and the bargain is invariably struck in private and care is taken that the secret does not leak out.

When Bhagwandas heard of his betrothal he was very much excited, but he was not at liberty to give expression to his feelings, for, in Indian society there is no appeal against a father's order. On the marriage day, the procession headed by the bridegroom marched to the bride's house and the marriage ceremony began. The family priest joined the hands of the husband and wife and asked the parents of the bride to give their daughter away. "We bestow the gift upon thee", uttered the parents of the bride simultaneously. Bhagwandas was then called upon to say in response, "I accept it with thanks"; but he would not say that; when pressed by the priest and his relatives to speak out the words, he angrily exclaimed, "I won't tell a lie; she is no gift; for, I have paid for her". No sooner were these words out of his mouth, than the parents of the bride hung down their heads with shame and the Kāyastha gentlemen present said things which had best remain unrecorded. They appealed to the honour of the bride's house and by persuasion not unaided by compulsion forced the guilty parents to repay the whole sum. This was done there and then. Bhagwandas had no objection now to say, "I accept the gift with thanks". He spoke the words and the bride became his forever.

Moral: We want boys and girls with sufficient stock of moral courage to say "ayes" and "nays" as they think proper. It behaves parents as well to look to the happiness of their children and be reasonable in exercising their despotic power. Unless and until we put a stop to the evil customs of early marriages, the sale of girls and the like, we should never hope to materially improve.

Story 81

If the Cap Fits, Wear It

There lived in a certain village a revenue Patel named Bhojo. He owned several acres of arable land and was a man of well-to-do circumstances. He understood the difference between "come" and "go" and therefore tilled his land in person, staying all day in the fields; and his wife Rādhā took him his midday meal consisting of *bājarī*-bread and onions, which he relished more than sumptuous dishes, after half a day's good work. The Patel and his wife had no children. The man's attention was therefore solely fixed on improving his land and the woman's in taking care of the produce thereof.

One year the Patel had sowed sesamum seeds in one of his fields and it gave him a good crop. The Patel brought the beans home when they were ripe and instructed his wife how to take out the seeds. While separating the seeds from the chaff, the woman helped herself freely to the *til* (sesamum), for, she liked it very much. Now, a calf, that was tied to a nail in the courtyard and had seen the woman eating the *til*, kept bleating all the time the Patel's wife ate the seeds. The woman took this to be an insult and was very much afraid lest it might betray her to her neighbours who would laugh at her and call her names for helping herself to the sesamum without her husband's knowledge. When therefore the Patel came home in the evening, she put on an aggrieved look and would not talk to him as was her wont. When the Patel lovingly asked her the reason, she said with tearful eyes, "This calf of yours watches my movements as if I wore a criminal. When I was eating a little of the sesamum seeds today, it went on blabbing all the while. If four neighbours come to know of it, they would jeer at me and take me for a thief. Either I or the calf must leave the house. We both can't live beneath the same roof." "I am ready to turn the insolent calf out," said the Patel, "but once in the streets it will blab out the secret all the more vigorously. An excellent idea strikes me. In the capacity of the headman of the village, I'll ask the public-crier to go from street to street and cry out as follows: "If the young calf tells you that the Patel's wife stole Till and ate it, don't believe it; for, it is false!" Rādhā was greatly pleased with the arrangement. She did not see that by justifying herself before the public she declared herself guilty.

Story 82

The Greatest Clerks are not Always the Wisest Men

In the old days when there were religious schools in Kāśī, Brahmin lads flocked there from all quarters to study Sanskrit, the mother of languages. The students were chiefly taught hundreds and thousands of [97] *śloka*s by heart, thus

[97] *Śloka*s = Sanskrit verses.

burdening the memory without an attempt at expanding the intellect. They would tell you everything about the [98]*svarga* and the *naraka*, but they knew next to nothing about the world they lived in. Again they were so proud of their sacred language that they would rather give up the ghost than utter a word of foreign origin. I remember to have read of a similar case in which a Parsi coaching clerk was asked by an orthodox Brahmin to sell him "a valuable piece of paper for Bombay" meaning a ticket for which there is no word in the Sanskrit language, for, there were unfortunately no Railways in the Vedic period. The clerk took him for a mad man and dealt him a blow on the nose. But that is another story; we had better keep to the one in hand.

A Brahmin lad of the above type was once going to a village in company with his Guru. Both master and pupil had a natural disgust for the [99]Prākr̥t and they spoke nothing but Sanskrit. The otherwise tedious journey on a summer day was enlivened by a lively discussion on the origin and roots of certain words every one of which occupied half an hour at least in being traced home. By midday they arrived at a well. The *guru* at once wont up the margin, perhaps to gauge the water; but either to make sure of its depth or to quench his thirst, he fell into it head downwards. The water fortunately was not deep, so he could keep his head above the water without much inconvenience. When the disciple saw his *guru* fall into the well, he cried out at the top of his voice; but he did so in Sanskrit, for, Prākr̥t he would not speak even to save his own life; "My *guru* has fallen

---

98 The *svarga* and the *naraka* = The upper and nether worlds; the heaven and hell.

99 Prākr̥t = Language derived from Sanskrit and spoken by low class people.

into the well; run, people, run!" There were several people working in the fields close by, but they did not mind him, for, they understood not a word of what he said. The *guru* who was very much shaken by the fall heard him and said, "Speak to them in Prākr̥t, or they will never come". The boy did so. The cultivators responded to his call and helped to draw the pot-bellied priest out of the well.

Moral: Learn to accommodate yourself to the time and circumstances in which you live.

Story 83

A Little Learning is a Dangerous Thing

According to the present standard of education prevailing in India, a student is required to pass in a variety of subjects. The natural result of this faulty process is that a student tries to learn something of everything and that something is too little to be of any practical use to him in the world and at times proves dangerous.

A student named Parbho once picked up in the course of a lecture that the sun, the moon, the stars, the earth and what not had no substantial supports to keep them from falling, but were kept in their places by the force of attraction. He had also learnt that a ball when thrown up falls back on the ground and does not keep in the air or go heavenwards, because it is nearer the earth than heaven and the earth being the greater body of the two possesses greater attractive power than the ball. If it were otherwise, the earth would fly to the hall and where we should all be in that case it is difficult to guess.

Parbho's father who was an astrologer of good repute was once summoned by a rich Baniā to read his horoscope. After examining the position and influence of every planet, the astrologer advised his patron to give a [100]*sīdhā* to a Brahmin for the pacification of Saturn and to take only one meal on Saturdays. The Baniā naturally asked the [101]Jośī to send his son for the *sīdhā*.

When Parbho was returning home with flour, sugar, rice and pulse tied at four corners of his kerchief and a pot of *ghee* in his hand a question rose in his mind. He asked himself which of the two — *ghee* or pot — had the greater power of attraction. The experiment must be made at any cost. He held the pot bottom upwards and both *ghee* and pot went severally down, thus proving at least that the earth had the greatest attraction of the three! On his return home his father further proved to him that his back had great attraction for a stick!

Moral: Learning makes a good man better and an ill man worse; for, the higher the ape goes, the more he shows his tail.

---

[100] *Sīdhā* = Quantity of flour, sugar, rice, pulse and *ghee* sufficient for one man.

[101] Jośī = An astrologer.

Story 84

Borrowing 5,000 Rupees on a Single Hair!

There lived in Ahmedabad a merchant named Tekchand, who was a man of means and credit and had earned an excellent reputation as an honest dealer. Once he "had" occasion to go to Rangoon to purchase rice. He had with him Rs. 10,000 in Bank Notes. The rates he thought were very profitable to him and he consequently bought a larger quantity than he could pay for. When the sellers called upon him for payment, he made calculations and found that he required Rs. 5,000 more to fully pay up their bills. Requesting the merchants to wait for an hour, he went to the bazaar and asked a banker to accomodate him with Rs. 5,000 which he said he would remit to him with interest within a month. The banker naturally asked him for a reference, but Tekchand explained to him that he was there for the first time in his life and was therefore not known to anybody. "I want the sum on my own credit, if you can advance it", he added. "But you must give me some sort of assurance that you can and will repay the sum", replied the banker.

"I give you my word of honour that I will repay the sum within a month. What further assurance can I give you in a foreign place where nobody knows me?" Asked Tekchancd.

"If you can't do that, have you any objection to mortgaging a hair of your mustache for the sum?" Suggested the banker.

Pulling out a hair from his mustache and giving it to the banker, Tekchand said, "Keep it in safe custody, sir, for, I will send for it in a few days". The banker after examining the hair, said, "This hair is crooked; let me have a straight one instead". "Crooked or not crooked makes very little difference", cried out Tekchand who was much enraged at seeing his hair slighted; "You will have to return it soon. Will you advance the sum on it?" The banker was convinced beyond a shadow of doubt that Tekchand was an honourable man and he forthwith complied with his request. Tekchand, of course, returned the money in duo time.

This hair story travelled from place to place and everybody admired Tekchand's self-respect and honourable conduct. An adventurer of little means and less reputation at once proceeded to Rangoon to try the experiment and enrich himself if it succeeded. He went to the same banker's shop and demanded a large sum on credit. The banker asked him for a hair of his mustache which he gave very willingly. When, however, the banker demanded another, on the plea that the one he gavc him was crooked, he pulled out another and offered it to him without exhibiting slightest offence. The banker coolly asked him to walk away, telling him that he would not advance a pie to a man who had no regard for his mustache.

Moral: Respcct thyself and thou wilt win the respect of others. The best title of a man to the respect of others must be founded on his own actions.

Honour is like the eye which cannot suffer the least impurity without damage; it is a precious stone the price of which is lessened by the least flaw.

Story 85

Weak Threads United Form a Strong Rope

One night a thief broke into the house of a Baniā and laid hands on the strong box, but before he could break it open, the Baniā woke up. Without giving an alarm or losing his presence of mind! he at once got up and approaching the thief with folded arms, he prostrated himself at his feet and said, "I know you are my family god and have come to bless me; for, your face exactly resembles that of the image I saw in a dream last night. You will, I pray, let me perform your *pūjā* and feed you with sweetmeats. Consider this house with everything it contains to be your own and me your humble slave?" The thief was mightily pleased with the reception, inwardly laughing at the Baniās credulity. He commanded the Baniā to make preparations for his *pūjā* without losing time, as he must be back before daybreak, he said. The Baniā awoke his wife and asked her to bring redpowder, rice, sugar, incense and all the necessary articles of *pūjā*.

He then prayed the thief to stand near a pillar and allow him to walk round him for 108 times with cotton-thread in hand. The thief did not object to it, for, he knew that circumambulation formed a part of the *pūjā*. At the end of each round the Baniā prostrated himself at his feet and invoked a blessing. One hundred and eight threads one over the other formed a strong rope and at the end of the *pūjā* the thief found himself securely fastened to the pillar. He asked the Baniā to untie the bond, but the latter calmly replied, "That's the work of the watchmen who will soon be here!" so saying he summoned the police and handed over the thief to them.

Moral: Never draw your dirk when a dunt will do.

Story 86

Vain Glory Blossoms but Never Bears

There lived in Halvad a Brahmin named Jaṭāśaṅkar who once had occasion to go to Ahmedabad accompanied by his son who was ten years old. A [102]*dhotar* hardly reaching the knee, a shirt covered all over with patches, a rope-like ragged turban and a thick coarse woollen blanket, constituted the Brahmin's dress. On one shoulder he carried a bag containing cooking utensils and brass gods and from the other was suspended a [103]*tūmbḍī* with a cotton string for drawing water from the wayside wells.

On the third day of their stay in Ahmedabad, a rich Brahmin invited all his caste-fellows to a grand dinner. From 3 o'clock in the afternoon, guests began to pour in. Almost all of them had on silken *dhotar*s with gold borders, silken kerchiefs thrown across their shoulders, rings encircling their arms and fingers and gold and pearl chains worn round their necks. They carried in their hands brass [104]*loṭā*s filled with drinking water.

It was some time before Jaṭāśaṅkar found the place and he was therefore among the latecomers. He had his coarse blanket wrapt round the loins and this shabby exterior together with

[102] *Dhotar* = A loincloth.

[103] *Tūmbḍī* = A hollow gourd for holding water.

[104] *Loṭā* = A small water pot.

the *tūmbḍī* gave him a beggarly look. The Brahmins taking him to be one made him sit apart from themselves at some distance. Jaṭāśaṅkar felt himself slighted but kept quiet.

It took about an hour to serve sweetmeats and vegetables of various kinds. The gods of the earth were then requested by the host to do justice to the homely fare. Now there is this distinction between the caste-dinners of Gujarat and those of Kāṭhiāwāṛ that to the Kāṭhiāwāṛī Brahmins a copious flow of *ghee* is indispensable while they don't care much for vegetables. To the Gujarātīs, variety in food is more pleasing. Jaṭāśaṅkar's son naturally therefore asked his father when they would serve *ghee*. To this he gravely replied, "These people don't like *ghee* very much, for, it is a costly thing. We are not now in our own Kāṭhiāwāṛ; where on occasions like this they spend with both hands. These Gujarātīs are a very miserly set of people." This was overheard by a Brahmin sitting near them and he sarcastically remarked, "Mahārāj, the frog cannot live out of her bog. It's no wonder you don't like these things, for, you have probably novel seen them in your lifetime, much less tasted them. Again, beggars should not be choosers. But where do you come from, my friend?" I come from Halvad in Kāṭhiāwāṛ," replied Jaṭāśaṅkar, "and I know best what our Kāṭhiāwāṛī dinners are like. You people prepare a great many vegetables, for they cost very little. We people use more *ghee* on occasions like this than you will use water!" "Talking is cheap, my friend; your very look bespeaks generosity," retorted the Brahmin.

Now this seemingly poor Brahmin of Halvad was a rich man. He was stung to the heart and he was not a man to quietly pocket the insult. When, therefore, the Brahmins rose to depart, he purposely placed his *tūmbḍī* in their way where it was soon crushed under foot and broken to pieces. At this, Jaṭāśaṅkar sat down in the middle of the road and began to mourn, as he said, for the death of his *tūmbḍī*! The other Brahmins gathered round him and offered to buy him a brass *loṭā* if that would satisfy him. "I would not have cared if it had been stolen; but now that it has died, I fear I shall have to perform its funeral ceremonies and feed the whole caste on the 13th day after its death!" he exclaimed. He then sent for a [105]*huṇḍī* from his native place and cashed it in Ahmedabad. On the 13th day, he invited all the Brahmins of the place and fed them with [106]*kansāra* and *ghee*. He instructed the waiters to serve *ghee* without reserve. The dinner cost him about Rs. 4,000, but at the same time it humbled the Gujarātī Brahmins forever.

Moral: India is sadly lacking in well organized charitable institutions. They would spend thousands on death and marriage occasions and would even incur debts to meet the extravagant expenses, but if you ask them to join and start an asylum for the old and diseased, or to establish scholarships, you would find them very close-fisted. Their charity is misdirected and they don't know how to make the right use of money.

Story 87

A Knife in the Box

An old Baniā named Nemchand dealt in a variety of drugs and enjoyed a very good custom. To save himself the trouble of opening the cash box every now and then,

105 *Huṇḍī* = A bill of exchange.

106 *Kansāra* = A kind of sweetmeat made of wheat flour and molasses.

he had cut two holes on the lid large enough for the silver and copper coins to glide in. In this box, he also kept a pen-knife which he frequently required for mending his reed-pens.

Once when the druggist was mending his pen, a customer came in with a long list of drugs to buy. He asked the Baniā to attend to him at once, for, the drugs, he said, had to be decocted and administered to a relative of his whose life was in poril. The druggist put the pen aside and thrust the knife with open blade into the box.

As usual he carried the box home at night and put it under his bedstead as was his wont. At about midnight, he suddenly woke up and began to say to himself, "I was really a fool to leave the knife open; suppose the bedstead is turned upside down by an earthquake or the tape gives way, I am sure to fall upon the box underneath. The lid might break and the knife I have left open might enter my body and the wound might prove fatal! I thank my stars that it is not too late yet." So saying he got up from the bed and opening the box he carefully closed the knife and then quietly went to bed again.

Moral: This is an extreme case and may not have come to pass at all, yet, men ought not to shut their eyes against the threatened danger and pursue them own course till the possibility of prevention has passed away.

Cf. "After wits are dearly bought"; "Let thy foreit guide thy thought".

Cf. "The swallow and other birds" — *Aesop's Fables.*

Story 88

Sītā [107]Haraṇa (Abduction of Sītā)

Once upon a time, a Brahmin came to the village of Rājpur. He was an excellent story-teller and knew the whole of the *Rāmāyaṇa* by heart; so the villagers met in a public place every night to hear the *kathā*. They were quite incapable of following the poetical descriptions of the Brahmin. Only a few among them could grasp enough to follow the main thread of the narrative.

There was a Patel with more of faith than common sense who regularly attended these nocturnal meetings. After a continuous narration of over two months they came to the chapter of Sītā-Haraṇa. The story-teller related the incident with much pathos and produced a very sad impression upon the minds of the audience. The Patel felt much for poor Rāma whose wife Sītā, he thought, was transformed into a *haraṇa* (deer)! He cursed Rāvaṇa for transforming a human being into a beast and heartily wished she might assume her human form before long. He was so much affected that he passed a sleepless night. Next morning he left for a neighbouring village where he had some business. When a couple of days later he came back and went to the meeting at night, the first question he put to the story-teller was this, "Before you proceed further tell me whether Sītā is still a *haraṇa* (deer) or has resumed her human form?" The whole audience laughed at his simplicity and the story-teller explained to him that "*Haraṇa* meant abduction and not a deer in that particular place".

---

[107] *Haraṇa* means abduction as well as a deer.

Moral: "It were better," says Lord Bacon, "to have no opinion of God at all than such an opinion as is unworthy of Him."

Story 89

Bobbing the Robbers

As a Baniā's [108]*jān* were going from the bride's house to the bridegroom's native place which was a few miles distant, they were waylaid by several robbers. As is the custom, the Baniās had their best clothes and costliest jewels on for this joyous occasion. They were stopped in the middle of the road and peremptorily asked to give up all they had.

The bridegroom who was an ingenuous young man was equal to the occasion. He got down from the bullock cart with his little bride by his side and pointing to the marriage knot he said, "This knot tied at the time of performing the marriage ceremony can only be untied before our family Goddess and we have to perform a regular ceremony accompanied by music and dancing before we do so. Dire calamity befalls everyone who disregards this or interferes with its performance. You will therefore allow us to perform the ceremony at the end of which everything will be handed over to you." The robbers who happened to be votaries of Kālī readily agreed to the proposal.

The Baniās then took off their clothes and assumed various garbs, some of males and the others of females, of different castes. They borrowed the robbers' trousers and sticks to play

[108] *Jān* = A marriage party.